Tea

Tea

RECIPES FOR HEALTH, WELLBEING AND TASTE

Margaret Roberts

NEW HOLLAND

CONTENTS

INTRODUCTION

Through the years I have found certain herbs to be absolutely remarkable in their effective, quick, and often astonishing relief of many a common ailment. Making an infusion of the fresh, organically grown plant, and sipping it quietly and slowly, often does more to ease the condition than a lot of serious medication, and I have proved this over and over again—but you still need to consult your doctor before starting a home treatment.

Children respond particularly well to herbal teas, as do animals. Often one can include the teas in a favourite fruit juice, or, in the case of animals, add it to their drinking water or mix it into their food. Generally people wrinkle their noses at the thought of a herbal tea, but if it is well made and sweetened, if liked, with a little honey, it is not only delicious but so quick to bring relief that one can become quite fanatical about the wonders of herbal teas! I certainly am, and very rarely drink any other form of tea.

Through my many years of experimenting, I have come to a number of comforting conclusions about herbal teas, which I share with you in this little book.

I wrote my first tea book in 1999. This proved to be so popular with so many requests from not only the students who attend my classes at the Herbal Centre, but also from the ever-increasing number of herb lovers. So here it is with added extras and new herbs included. I have also included a special recipe for each herb that you can try for a different and exciting taste experience.

There isn't space to go into the growing of these precious plants, but *Starting Out With Herbs*, also published by New Holland, covers any other queries you may have. Most garden centres and health food shops will be able to supply the herbs and spices found in this book. There are many online herbs suppliers you can search on the internet who will deliver to you.

Margaret Roberts

What is tea?

Tea is a hot drink made from a blend of or one type of dried or fresh leaves, and can have spices, juices and fruits added. It is normally made in a pot, or it can be made in a jug or straight into the cup. Western cultures tend to separate tea into those drinks made with the tea plant, and those we call herbal infusions.

The earliest recorded tea usage was in 350 AD, when a Chinese dictionary cited tea for the first time as 'Erh Ya'.

Camellia sinensis: the tea plant

The leaves of tea from this plant is the world's most popular beverage, and yet no one thinks of tea in its many forms as a herb, even though it has been used in Chinese medicine for 5000 years! The dried leaves are the most popular variety amongst Western drinkers. Perhaps this is because black tea blends are more suited to the addition of milk and sugar.

Chinese leaves produce Keemun, Lapsang Souchong, Oolong and Yunnan teas. Most Chinese tea drinkers do not add milk or sugar.

In India, the best-known teas are Darjeeling and Assam and Nilgiri. Ceylon is a light tea with crisp citrus undertones.

The most common blended black teas for Western drinkers include English Breakfast, Earl Grey and Irish Breakfast.

Chai is popular also, and is black tea that is brewed strong with a combination of spices and diluted with milk and sugar.

HERBAL INFUSIONS

Herbal infusions are comprised of fresh or dried herbs, spices, roots, seeds or flowers that are infused in hot water. Most herbal infusions are caffeine free.

How to make the perfect cup of herbal tea

Try and use the fresh leaves or flowers for the best tea. The easiest way to obtain these is from your own garden! However, you can also find these in nurseries, from herbal tea specialists and herbs and spices shops, many of which can be ordered online.

Dried herbs and spices can also be used to make these recipes. Just use the same quantities. The standard brews for herbal teas are as follows:

When using leaves and flowers:
Take a ¼ cup fresh leaves and/or flowers. Pour over this 1 cup of boiling water, allow to draw for three to five minutes, then strain. Sip slowly.

When using bark and seeds:
1–2 teaspoons seed approximately, e.g. aniseed. 1 tablespoon bark, e.g. cinnamon. Pour over this 1 cup of boiling water, allow to draw for five minutes, then strain.

Doses for children:
½ cup or even ¼ cup, and for a baby 2 teaspoons at a time. Lemon balm, chamomile and fennel are invaluable children's herbs.

Doses for animals: Add 1 cup of strained herbal tea to 2 cups of water in their water bowls or mix ½ –1 cup of herb tea into their food.

Never use any plant as a tea unless you are 100% sure of its identification. Many plants are poisonous; in some cases certain parts of a plant may be edible, while other parts may be poisonous. When in doubt, leave out.

THE BENEFITS OF
LEMON AND HONEY

Both lemon and honey can be added to most of the herbal teas in this book. Both are hugely important in the building of health, and honey is the best natural sweetener ever known to humankind.

Honey is a wonderful unwinding, calming, soothing and relaxing addition to herbal tea.

Honey contains a mass of mineral salts, amino acids, vitamins and natural, easily digested sugars. Honey is a sleep inducer and a natural disinfectant and painkiller. It is surprisingly often used as a country remedy spread onto open sores, scratches and grazes—many a horse has had a honey wound dressing that the vet has recommended. (Manuka honey is particularly reknown for this property.)

Honey has antibacterial and antiviral properties, and it helps to ease diarrhoea, asthma and sore throats. (The old-fashioned sage tea with honey and lemon is still one of the most popular sore-throat treatments today.)

Lemon, with its vitamin C, has been used for centuries as a cold remedy, and it also soothes the stomach. Lemon adds a fresh flavour to herbal tea.

Important
Health Notes

Always be sure before starting a home treatment that you consult your doctor—these herbal teas are in no way meant to replace the doctor, or any medication you are on.

It is always safest to use one individual herb at a time, as mixing the herbs often dissipates their efficacy. However, although it is advisable to drink only one cup of a specific herbal tea a day, you can drink several cups of different herbal teas throughout the day.

During an acute illness, for example flu or a cold, you can take a specific herb three to four times during the day to ease the condition, but a general rule is to take only one of a kind daily, then after ten days give it a break of three or four days, then continue, stopping every ten days for three to four days, before continuing.

Herbs are far more powerful than we realise and can accumulate within the body. So it is best to take a variety and also to take them in moderation.

Very importantly, all herbs must be organically grown with no chemical fertilisers or sprays whatsoever, as the herb is immediately absorbed by the body and it needs to be 100 per cent pure. Also, be sure that no irradiated spices or seeds are used, and never dry the herbs in a microwave. It is best to use herbs fresh, but in case you have to dry them do so by hanging them up, or spread them on newspaper in the shade and turn daily. Store dried herbs in a screw-top glass bottle and don't keep them for longer than three months. After that they're not even palatable.

Above all, enjoy this remarkable way of absorbing the health-giving properties of nature's little miracles. Herbs make all the difference to our health and state of mind; they lift our spirits and give us never-ending interest. Relish every sip!

ANISE

Pimpinella anisum

Anise is a pretty, quick-growing little annual and the whole plant–flowers included–makes a deliciously comforting tea, and the seeds (aniseed) have been treasured through the centuries as a medicine.

One of the best digestive herbs, aniseed has been used to treat heartburn, sour belching, wind, colic and nausea. It will quickly ease hiccoughs, dissipate bloating and is a superbly effective antispasmodic, countering and soothing menstrual cramps, spasmodic tight coughing, whooping cough, bronchitis, pneumonia and heat prostration.

Many a nursing mother has sipped cups of aniseed tea to increase her breast milk production (which benefits the baby's colic too). CAUTION: Do not take anise in any form during pregnancy.

New research is finding that anise tea is beneficial in treating frigidity and impotence and for the easing of the menstrual cycle. The ancient Greeks used aniseeds and fresh flowers for pain relief and recorded that aniseed warms, dries, dissolves, facilitates breathing, provokes urine, eases thirst and relieves pain–and modern research verifies this.

Make a tea of 2 teaspoons of aniseeds, pour over this 1 cup of boiling water, leave it to stand for four to five minutes, give it a good stir, then either strain and sip slowly, or chew the seeds well with the tea–they are delicious.

Alternatively, make a tea of fresh leaves and flowers by steeping 1/4 cup of the leaves and flowers in 1 cup of boiling water for three to four minutes. Strain, sweeten with a touch of honey, if liked, and sip slowly.

The cooled tea made of either the fresh flowers and leaves, or the seeds, can also be strained and used as a lotion or wash for oily skin, enlarged pores and acne, and in a spray bottle misted over the face will help to freshen, brighten and remove oiliness and redness, and to give an instant moisturising effect to a hot flushed face.

Basil

Ocimum basilicum species

There is an incredible variety of tastes in this popular group of herbs and although most are quick annuals like the delicious lemon basil, cinnamon basil, Thai basil, ginger basil and Genoese basil, it is to the perennial sacred basil, Ocimum basilicum sanctum (now called Ocimum basilicum tenuifolium) that I most often turn, not only for its rich clove-like scent and taste, but for its instant antispasmodic effect.

I try to have a cup of sacred basil tea almost every day and grow a bush or two at the kitchen door for quick pickings, as it is thought to be beneficial for the heart in particular. Research in India, its native land, has found it to be helpful in lowering high blood pressure, cleansing the blood, and lowering blood sugar and cholesterol levels. It is regarded as an 'adaptogenic', which helps the body to cope with, and adapt to, new bombardments of stress and tension-filled demands, and it acts as a tonic, energising and restoring the balance.

I also grow the huge sprawling 'High Hopes Basil'–the biggest of all the basils, with its mass of flowers which can be included in the tea, and add a jug full of tea to my bath water to experience that lovely, so needed relaxation while I sip slowly …

All the basils have excellent detoxifying and anti-inflammatory effects, and even chewing a leaf will ease indigestion and tension, and sipping a cup of basil tea is a most soothingly pleasant experience.

Take 1/4 cup of fresh leaves (never even think of using dried basil–it loses virtually all its taste in the drying), pour over this 1 cup of boiling water, leave it to stand for three to five minutes, strain and sip slowly.

Basil tea is also an excellent slimmer's tea, and is more and more popular today for 'the detox process', particularly after a calorie-rich meal. Sacred basil tea is effective for bladder ailments, acne, over-oily skin and blemishes and to stimulate circulation, to name but a few uses, and it is a much loved 'cure-all' in its diversity. Try it!

Aniseed and Orange Winter Warmer

Serves 2

2 teaspoons aniseed
orange zest
1 cup freshly squeezed orange juice
2 teaspoons honey

Pour 1 cup of boiling water over the aniseed and a twist of orange zest. Stand for 5 minutes. Simmer the orange juice with honey for 1 minute. Stir to dissolve the honey. Add the aniseed tea to the pot of orange juice and stir for 1 minute. Strain. Sip slowly to take the chill away and to soothe a tired throat.

BASIL REVIVER

At the end of a hot afternoon this is a
superb cool refresher.

1/4 cup fresh basil leaves
6 thin slices unpeeled cucumber
2 thick slices peeled pineapple

Pour 1 cup of boiling water over 1/4 cup of fresh
basil leaves. Stand for 3 minutes, strain and
pour into a glass. Stand this in a bowl and tuck
ice around it. While it cools whirl 6 thin slices of
unpeeled cucumber and 2 thick slices of peeled
pineapple in a liquidiser. Add 2 tablespoons of
crushed ice. Mix in the basil tea and serve in a tall
glass with more crushed ice.

BERGAMOT

Bee balm Monarda didyma

Known as Oswego tea by the American Indians, this gloriously rich-flavoured tea has been around for centuries. It eases nausea, vomiting and digestive upsets, and soothes coughs and colds and nasal congestion, and helps to dry up mucous and clear sinuses.

It has antiseptic and anti-inflammatory properties and is a quickly-soothing digestive and decongestant that is a pleasure to drink.

Take ¼ cup of fresh leaves and flowers, pour over this 1 cup of boiling water and stand it for five minutes. Then strain, sweeten with a touch of honey and add a squeeze of lemon juice, specially for a cough and cold, and sip slowly.

The arresting flavour and fragrance of bergamot tea is similar to that of the Italian bergamot orange, Citrus bergamia, which gives Earl Grey tea its distinctive taste and, by adding two fresh bergamot leaves to a pot of ordinary tea, you can immediately get that Earl Grey flavour and achieve the wonderful easing of tension and release of anxiety by the third sip.

Cooled tea can be used as a soothing face wash for oily problem skin and is remarkably effective in a spritz bottle sprayed frequently onto the skin to cool and clear away pollution build-up and to refresh in midsummer heat.

A cup of bergamot tea has been taken through centuries to treat kidney ailments, to help flush out toxins, to ease bronchitis and insomnia and even backache, and new medical research in America is proving it's not just a pretty garden perennial. It really is an extraordinary plant and tough and easy to grow so far from its native habitat.

Try the cooled tea with fruit juice as a summer refresher. It's addictive!

BORAGE

Borago officinalis

Borage is a fabulously mineral-rich herb that grows quickly and abundantly in every type of soil, and it reseeds so easily you are never without it.

The exquisite star-like flowers can be added to the tea of prickly cucumber-tasting leaves, ¼ of a cup, and with 1 cup of boiling water poured over it, its immediately refreshing store of minerals is released. Stand for five minutes, then strain and add a touch honey or a squeeze of lemon juice, stir with a cinnamon stick and sip slowly.

Borage is an extraordinary anti-ager, and it stimulates the adrenal cortex to produce its own cortisone. It acts as a natural diuretic, it has anti-rheumatic properties and is a superb expectorant.

Rich in vitamins and particularly calcium, borage tea is an excellent cough treatment and expectorant, clearing the chest of phlegm and easing spasms of coughing and soothing and lessening the coughing gently and effectively.

Borage is one of the best herbs to ease irritable bowel syndrome, it regulates menstruation and it contains gamma-linoleic acid, a remarkable anti ager.

Our grandmothers used the cooled borage tea as a face wash and as a rinse for the hair after shampooing and found it useful for restoring flaky dry skin on the face and scalp.

Borage tea should not be taken every day over long periods as it is so mineral rich. So take it for eight to ten days and give it a break of a week, then take it for eight to ten days, and so on.

This was the herb the Crusaders took on their journeys to give them courage, joy and gladness, along with yarrow to stop bleeding. Today we face other kinds of crusades and borage does the trick!

BERGAMOT EARL GREY SPICY TEA

The best experience is to sip this very slowly on an autumn afternoon as the first chill sets in and you can pick the last of the season's bergamot leaves before it dies down for winter.

1 Earl Grey tea bag
2 bergamot leaves
1 cinnamon stick
1 lemon slice
cinnamon powder
1 fresh lemon slice
honey to taste

Pour 1 cup of boiling water over Ceylon tea bag and 2 bergamot leaves, 1 cinnamon stick and 1 lemon slice. Remove the tea bag after 10–15 seconds. Stand for 5 minutes and stir frequently with the cinnamon stick. Strain, pour into a pretty mug, and add a sprinkling of cinnamon powder, a fresh lemon slice and a touch of honey.

BORAGE PARTY CUP

Serves 6

This was one of the 19th-century court drinks

2 cups of borage leaves and flowering tops
6 slices of lemon
juice of 1 lemon
6 cloves
2 cups of unsweetened apple juice
½ teaspoon of powdered cloves
4 teaspoons honey

Cover borage leaves and flowering tops with 4 cups of boiling water. Add slices of lemon, the lemon juice and cloves. Stand for 5 minutes. Strain and cool. Add unsweetened apple juice, powdered cloves and honey. Mix well. Serve with ice and float a few borage flowers on top.

CALENDULA

Calendula officinale

This bright and cheerful winter annual is one of the world's most loved healing plants and for this alone every garden should be filled with calendulas in the cold months–the dried petals can be stored in screw-top glass jars for use during the rest of the year.

Take 1 fresh flower, pour over it 1 cup of boiling water and let it stand for five minutes. Strain, sweeten with a touch of honey, if liked, and sip slowly.

Calendula tea is used to treat gum problems, mouth ulcers, after tooth extraction, to relieve indigestion–sip frequently at intervals. As a liver tonic, calendula has been effectively used for centuries.

The cooled and unsweetened tea can be used as a superb face wash for spotty oily skin and teenage acne, and a cup of calendula tea taken daily has proved to help skin and scalp problems reliably through the years, even cooled tea in a spray bottle makes a superb skin freshener and lotion if applied several times through the day with toning and quick-healing results–much loved by actresses who had calendula tea in their dressing rooms always!

It is fascinating to know that through the centuries calendula tea has been used to treat sore nipples while breastfeeding and rough rashes and itchy allergy areas on the skin, nappy rash and chilblains, haemorrhoids, varicose veins and leg ulcers.

Research has found that calendula has antiseptic and antibacterial properties and that it was used in eye baths and as poultices over the eyes to help cataracts and to soothe red tired sore eyes as long as three centuries ago.

The tea can be added to aqueous cream to make a soothing healing cream, and modern cosmetics make use of this remarkable plant with often astonishing results.

This is one annual I'm never without!

CALENDULA WINTER TREAT

To shake off the chill and soothe a sore throat.

¼ cup of fresh calendula petals
2 teaspoons of fresh mandarin peel
1 teaspoon of molasses or thick dark honey
2 tablespoons of fresh mandarin juice
sprinkling of cayenne pepper

Steep calendula petals in 1 cup of boiling water with fresh mandarin peel for 5 minutes. Add molasses or thick dark honey and fresh mandarin juice. Stir well, strain and add a small sprinkling of cayenne pepper. Sip slowly, slowly. You'll warm up in a minute—and your throat will be soothed as well.

CARAWAY

Carum carvi

Caraway surely has to be one of the world's most well-known digestives! Just a few little seeds chewed can ease indigestion, searing heartburn, flatulence, colic, nausea, bloating and cramps. It is a natural antispasmodic and the chewed seeds sweeten the breath and relieve gripes and tummy rumblings. With a cup of caraway tea life becomes altogether more pleasant.

Make a tea with ¼ cup fresh leaves and flowering heads and some seeds. Pour over this 1 cup of boiling water and stand for five minutes, then strain and sip slowly. Alternatively, take 1 teaspoon of seeds, pour 1 cup of boiling water over them, stand for five minutes and sip slowly, chewing the seeds.

The seeds also have a reputation of increasing breast milk production in nursing mothers, and this will also help to ease the baby's wind and colic and tenseness.

Interestingly, caraway tea was given by monks in medieval times as a treatment for fear, anxiety, grief and terror and for spasms and pain, and they grew the precious little plant in their cloister gardens. The soldiers going off on battle would take with them a little pouch, made of leather and filled with caraway seeds, which could hang from their belts.

Today many restaurants in Europe and the Middle East still serve a small bowl of caraway seeds, sometimes mixed with cumin seeds, fennel seeds and aniseeds, to ease digestion after a heavy meal–just a pinch in the mouth slowly chewed does wonders, and a cup of caraway tea, unsweetened, is the most delicious way of ending a meal.

The ancient Egyptians used caraway in their medicines, and seeds found in brass boxes in the tombs show that caraway was regarded as worth taking into the afterlife.

CARDAMOM

Elettaria cardamomum

Cardamom is another precious ancient spice with an exquisite flavour. The seeds are a superb digestive, easing colic, flatulence and gripes and sweetening the breath. A tea of cardamom seeds after a heavy, garlic-rich meal, will help to remove the smell and digest it effortlessly. Just a few seeds chewed will freshen the breath so beautifully, and as cardamom is an excellent tonic used throughout history as an antispasmodic, I often wonder why cardamom after-dinner sweets or even cardamom chewing gum have not been exploited.

First used by the early Egyptians and then later by the ancient Greeks and Romans, cardamom was a treasured spice which found its way into Europe and from there spread by way of the romantic caravan routes.

Much used in the Middle East and India, cardamom still is an expensive spice, and although it grows like ginger it remains virtually exclusive to the Malabar Coast of India, Sri Lanka and Guatemala.

Not only does cardamom make a beautiful cup of tea but it is better known as an after-dinner drink with coffee or with orange- or mandarin-rind tea. In the Middle East black espresso coffee is flavoured with cardamom, and crushed seeds are often added to mulled wine.

To make a cup of refreshing digestive cardamom tea, pour 1 cup of boiling water over 3 cardamom pods that have been lightly crushed–it's the small black seeds that hold the fragrant taste. Add a thin paring of lemon or orange rind and let it stand for five minutes. Sip it slowly. Green tea–1 teaspoon–can be added to this if liked. It's so refreshing you'll create your own recipes!

CARAWAY CALMER

To release anxiety, stress and tension, sip this wonder brew quietly and slowly.

2 teaspoons of caraway seeds
1 teaspoon of fennel seeds
a twist of lemon zest
2 teaspoons of honey
a pinch of allspice powder (pimento)
1 sprig of lemon balm (melissa)

Simmer 1 cup of water with caraway seeds, fennel seeds, a twist of lemon zest, honey and allspice powder (pimento) for 5 minutes. Strain and sip slowly. To ease that fluttering heart, add lemon balm (melissa) to the strained tea.

MY FAVOURITE CARDAMOM DRINK

To help you unwind and to soothe a troubled heart, this tea takes some beating.

3–5 cardamom pods, crushed
1–2 teaspoons of thinly-pared orange rind
2 teaspoons of dried or fresh chamomile
1 sprig of mint

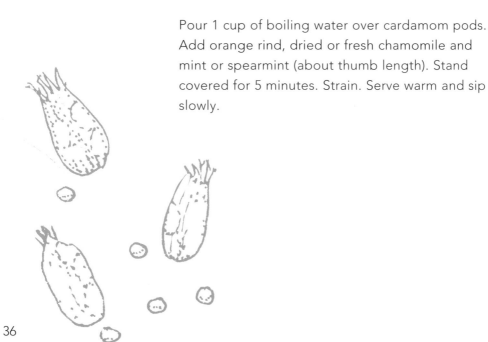

Pour 1 cup of boiling water over cardamom pods. Add orange rind, dried or fresh chamomile and mint or spearmint (about thumb length). Stand covered for 5 minutes. Strain. Serve warm and sip slowly.

CATMINT

Nepeta mussinii, N. cataria

Much loved by cats, catmint, or catnip, is an easy plant to grow in the garden and both the low-growing bluey-mauve-flowered smaller Nepeta mussinii and the bigger white-flowered Nepeta cataria make excellent teas.

It was drunk as a tea centuries before tea was even thought of and was so valuable a medication that every cottage gardener grew it.

This pungent-smelling and tasting herb will settle restlessness, soothe an upset tummy, remove gas, sour belchings, heartburn, colic and tummy rumblings, and it will unwind hyperactive, bed-wetting, yelling, over-excited little children. It will also lift and soothe a tension headache, ease indigestion and butterflies in the stomach, and smooth apprehension and anxiety and tenseness and delayed menstruation, as well as the aches and pains of arthritis, rheumatism and general muscle tension.

To make the tea, take ¼ cup fresh catnip sprigs, pour over this 1 cup of boiling water, leave it to stand for five minutes, then strain and sip slowly.

The cooled tea makes an excellent soothing lotion for haemorrhoids, rashes, scrapes, stings and grazes, and if the tea has a thumb-length sprig of fresh marjoram in it, and ½ a cup is given to a bed-wetting child before going to sleep, it will calm and soothe the child and greatly alleviate the bed-wetting problem. I find that ¼–½ a cup at mid-afternoon, sweetened with a little honey, and then ¼–½ a cup before bedtime, taken for ten days at a time, then given a break of two days before continuing, is a great help.

Catmint tea has the ability to increase a person's perspiration during a cold or flu, and it also, surprisingly, contains vitamin C.

CELERY

Apium graveolens

We really don't give celery the respect and admiration it deserves. It really is an awesome herb!

Native to Britain and Europe, celery has been revered, respected and cultivated from the earliest centuries as a food, a flavourant and a medicine. In those ancient days it was used to clear the body of toxins, excess fluid and poison, and to ease arthritic and rheumatic aches and pains.

Some 3 000 years ago ancient Egyptians ate celery to give them strong bones, strong muscles and fleetness of foot, and in the fifth century BC the ancient Chinese used celery to slow ageing and to treat many illnesses and flush toxins from the body.

The leaves, stems, flowers and seeds are used to treat chest ailments, lower blood pressure, and as a detoxifier of the bladder and kidneys, and celery will act as a urinary antiseptic, treat cystitis and improve circulation to the muscles and joints.

For gout, rheumatism and arthritis, celery taken both as a tea and as a fresh salad daily will dispose of the urates that cause the stiffness and pain, and reduce acidity in the body. It is a tonic, a toner, a detoxifier and a cleanser, and a precious sedative.

We need to sit up and take notice! Grow your own celery and reap the seeds for tea. Celery seed tea is made using 1 teaspoon of seeds to 1 cup of boiling water, stand for five minutes, sip slowly, chew the seeds.

New medical research finds celery has anti-convulcent properties and cooled celery tea is a superb lotion for problem oily skin! What a herb!

CATMINT WITH LEMON BALM

This is specially marvellous for overactive little children. Catmint and lemon balm have calming properties and work so well together.

1 thumb-length sprig of catmint
1 thumb-length sprig of lemon balm (melissa)
2 crushed cardamom pods
½ a cup of unsweetened pear juice
sprinkling of cinnamon powder
touch of honey

Take catmint, lemon balm (melissa) and cardamom pods. Pour over these 1 cup of boiling water. Stand for 5 minutes. Strain. Take ½ a cup and mix with unsweetened pear juice and add a sprinkling of cinnamon powder. Sweeten with the merest touch of honey and add crushed ice. Sit down and drink it slowly.

CELERY DETOX

This is a superb cleansing tea, especially for slimmers.

CAUTION: Do not take celery seed tea, nor eat a lot of celery, if you are pregnant or have a kidney disorder. Talk to your doctor first before starting a home treatment.

¼ cup of celery leaves
¼ cup of fennel leaves
1 teaspoon of celery seed
½ cup of carrot juice
10 cucumber slices
5 sprigs of parsley
juice of 1 lemon.

Pour 1 cup of boiling water over celery leaves and fennel leaves. Add celery seed. Stand for 5 minutes, strain and cool. Add carrot juice, cucumber and parsley, pushed through a juice extractor. Mix well. Add the lemon juice. Serve chilled. One glass a day works beautifully.

CHAMOMILE

Anthemis recutita

Chamomile has to be one of the world's favourite herbal teas! They've been making chamomile tea since the 4th century and from the 14th century onwards chamomile was a registered medicine!

It has the effect of soothing, calming and unwinding, it acts as a superb digestive, it eases stress, helps to treat insomnia, tension and terrible worry. It's a general and wondrous healing herb, and taken as a tea acts quickly and safely. For both the elderly and the young it's safe and comforting and has natural aspirin in it.

Made into a wash or a lotion, its soothing antiseptic qualities will quickly clean a graze or clear a rash, ease a bruise or sprain, and take the throbbing pain from haemorroids, ulcers and cuts.

The cooled tea will stop the itch and discomfort of eczema and clear up spotty skin affected by acne, and it can be applied as a lotion in a spritz bottle. You can gargle with the cooled tea, swish out the mouth to treat bleeding gums and mouth ulcers, or use it as a douche to clear up any itchy infections.

To make the tea, pour 1 cup of boiling water over 1/4 cup of either fresh flowers or just less of the dried flowers. Stand for five minutes, stir well, strain and sweeten with honey if liked.

Chamomile also has anti-inflammatory and antiseptic components, and so is used in registered modern medicines the world over. Research has isolated various remarkable compounds in it, like the precious deep blue azulene in its essential oil, and if that cup of chamomile tea poured around an ailing plant boosts it to health, imagine what it will do for us!

Chamomile will still be around for many decades to come. Let it become part of our stress-filled lives now!

CINNAMON

Cinnamomum species

Warming, fragrant, delicious and sweetly comforting, cinnamon is a much-loved spice all over the world.

An ancient custom was to stir a hot medicinal tea or a syrup or a mixture with a piece of cinnamon bark or a cinnamon stick, and, although we have largely forgotten that practice today, it will certainly impart its warming, relaxing, antispasmodic goodness to everything it touches.

Just a pinch of powdered cinnamon to a steaming cup of water flavoured with a squeeze or two or three of fresh lemon juice and sweetened with honey, is infinitely soothing and warming for a cold or chill, or a feeling of deep fatigue, or, as our grandmothers knew, to treat shock or an upsetting experience. Sipped slowly, it quickly works its magic.

Cinnamon has antibacterial qualities, and it is a superb antispasmodic—releasing fear, anxiety and despair gently and surely—and it acts as a warming tonic to the whole system.

Try bruising a thumb-length bit of cinnamon bark in a little honey and then adding a cup of boiling water. Sip slowly to ease a tight chest and wheezing, to soothe menopausal symptoms and that feeling of helplessness, and as a tonic for the kidneys and liver, without the honey.

Cinnamon trees grow in frost-free areas and the leaves too have that wonderful fragrance. Toss them into the bath while you lie back and sip your cinnamon tea! Cinnamon is excellent for the diabetic, talk to your doctor about it.

Note: Surprisingly, cinnamon is a uterine stimulant, so avoid it during pregnancy.

Classic Chamomile

Even at 3 a.m. when you wake anxious and drenched with worry, this cup of calm will help you to dip into sleep again. All four ingredients have soothing, calming and quietening qualities.

¼ cup of fresh or less of dried chamomile flowers

thumb-length sprig of lemon balm

3 allspice berries, lightly cracked

a little honey

Cover chamomile flowers with 1 cup of boiling water. Add lemon balm and allspice berries. Stand for 5 minutes. Strain. Add honey to sweeten and stir well. Sip slowly and feel the tension melt away.

CINNAMON SOOTHER

This tea definitely lightens the load and takes away that feeling of helplessness. Take it as a nightcap, unsweetened, for menopause symptoms.

1 cinnamon stick

1 teaspoon of caraway seeds

½ teaspoon of cumin seeds

Take cinnamon, caraway seeds and cumin seeds. Pour over this 1 cup of boiling water, stand for 5 minutes, covered, then strain. Sip slowly. Chew ½ a teaspoon of the discarded seeds–they will soothe the digestion.

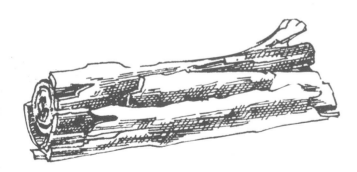

CORN SILK

Zea mays

This is always a surprise to herbal tea lovers. The silk inside the husk of an organically grown corn is so extraordinarily high in potassium that it soothes the lining of the entire urinary tract, eases prostate problems and relaxes the spasm and tension caused by frequent, difficult and very slow urination that is so often an indication of a prostate problem.

A tea of corn silk also flushes the kidneys and the bladder, and during an attack of cystitis is particularly soothing as it soothes the bladder lining and the lining of the urethra. It also helps to reduce kidney stone formation and has been used for centuries by the American Indians to treat chronic bladder infections in both men and women. For chronic cystitis it is one of the most comforting treatments (and for animals too) and the mealie silk or beard can be dried for teas during the winter months. Keep it sealed in a screw-top jar.

Should you suffer from frequent boils, mealie silk tea is extremely helpful in clearing the infection. The American Indians used the hot silk as a poultice after it had been drawn for the tea, on the area (cool until comfortable–test carefully first), held in place with a crepe bandage.

This bland and pleasant tea is also excellent for fluid retention and is safe to take during pregnancy, with the doctor's permission.

To make the tea, pour 1 cup of boiling water over 1/3 to ½ cup of the fresh silk (use ¼ cup of dried silk to the 1 cup of boiling water) and leave to draw for five minutes. Strain and drink up to five cups during the day if the condition is acute.

Every summer grow a row of mealies in the garden and reap the silk–it's an amazingly soothing and ancient medicine.

CLOVES

Eugenia catophyllata

I have always been intrigued by cloves–so tiny a little scrap of a bud with so intense a flavour, with such a huge a pain-killing effect, especially for tooth-ache, never ceases to astonish!

Cloves are the dried flower buds of one of the remarkable Eugenias. On my honeymoon the ship we sailed in anchored at Zanzibar in East Africa, and long before we even saw land, the scent of the drying cloves filled the sea air so exquisitely, I have never forgotten it. Ashore later, we walked between the great spreads of raked cloves drying in the sun on massive tarpaulins. The workers raked and re-raked all through the day to ensure an even drying process, and all had cloths tied over their noses and mouths so intense was the scent, and our clothes smelt of that delicious clove perfume for weeks afterwards.

From ancient times cloves have been made into a tea. The tea can be sipped slowly to reduce muscular aches and pains and spasms, to ease extreme tension and to eliminate parasites.

To make clove tea, place 10 cloves in a cup, bruise them lightly by pounding them in a little hot water for a minute, them fill up with 1 cup of boiling water and stir well.

Medical research through the decades has found cloves to have not only antispasmodic effects, but also analgesic effects, and that cloves have a mind-stimulating effect that improves memory, particularly after long illness or extremely stress-filled situations.

Newer research has found that cloves are helpful in treating acne, and that a pinch of ground cloves in the cooled tea can be an effective lotion, helping spotty, oily skin.

Through the centuries cloves have been regarded as a panacea for most ills, and with new research perhaps cloves will be a future cure-all!

CORN SILK TEA

Soothing, comforting and delicious, this gentle tea flushes the kidneys and soothes away the pains.

¼ cup of fresh or dried corn silk
3 thumb-length sprigs of thyme
1 teaspoon of fennel seeds
Squeeze of lemon juice

Pour 1 cup of boiling water over corn silk and thyme and fennel seeds. Stand for 5 minutes, stir well. Strain and add a squeeze of lemon juice. Sip slowly.

This is one of the most amazing of the herb teas and can be taken 2–4 times a day during a flare-up of an infection.

Red clover

Trifolium pratense

White clover

Trifolium repens

The humble clover, that pest in our lawns, is making strides in medical research and causing much interest. Both leaves and flowers are found to have exceptional components that show anti-inflammatory and anti-cancer effects.

Through the decades, a cup of clover tea was taken, sipped slowly to treat bronchitis, whooping cough, arthritis, gout, psoriasis and eczema, and as a treatment to soothe chronic cough and a postnasal drip. For the postnasal drip, clover tea was often combined with violet tea (see page 119). The cooled tea was used as a wash or lotion for psoriasis, eczema and sunburn.

To make clover tea, take 1/4 cup fresh leaves and flowers, pour over this 1 cup of boiling water, leave it to stand for five minutes, then strain.

The flowers of the red clover, particularly, are used in anti-cancer treatments, extracts are used in medicines and in creams for external application in skin cancers, and as both are so easy to grow we need to have them growing in our gardens for frequent cups of health-giving teas.

Once used extensively as a treatment for constipation, clover tea is still a favourite country remedy in Europe today, and a cup a day of winter tea made by combining rosehips, dried clover flowers, dried mint and honey, is still taken to ward off winter flu, chills and coughs, just as the medieval monks prepared it. As a bonus, clover plants dug back into the soil after flowering in autumn, will act as a superb enricher to poor soil.

Every part of the plant is precious. Plant some today—it will thrive in any soil in full sun!

Clover, Lemon and Sage Tea for Coughs

1/3 cup of clover flowers

rind of ½ a lemon

10 cloves

¼ cup of sage leaves

2 teaspoons honey

Simmer clover flowers, rind, cloves and sage leaves in 2 cups of water for 8 minutes. Strain. Add juice of lemon and honey. Drink ½ a cup warmed 4 times throughout the day. Sip slowly.

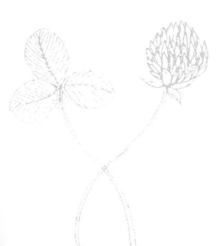

Cloves and Sage

During exam times or times of stress, this remarkable tea will boost the memory cells so astonishingly you'll be happily surprised!

4 sage leaves

10 cloves

a slice of lemon

dusting of powdered cloves

teaspoon of honey

Take sage and cloves. Pour over this 1 cup of boiling water and stand for 5 minutes. Crush it all with the spoon during that time. Then strain. Add lemon, powdered cloves and honey. Sip slowly. Take 1 cup a day or even 2 if necessary during exams, then stop. It's powerful!

COMFREY

Symphytum officinale

Comfrey is one of the world's most ancient and most amazing healing herbs. It contains the substance allantoin, a cell proliferator that repairs damaged tissue and bone, and it was once known as 'knitbone'.

The roots contain the most allantoin and also contain the pyrrlizidene alkaloids, which can cause liver damage if taken in excess–remember to always consult your doctor before starting a home treatment.

To make the tea, use comfrey leaves–1/4 cup of chopped leaf to 1 cup of boiling water, stand for three to five minutes, then strain, and take only 1 cup a day for ten days, then stop. Comfrey tea helps to ease bruises, sprains, boils, fractures, torn ligaments, aching arthritic joints, gout, pneumonia, productive bronchitis and coughs, rheumatism and fungal skin infections.

It is without doubt one of the most incredible healing plants known to mankind, and a lotion made of the cooled tea will help to heal wounds, ulcers, bed sores, grazes, rashes and infected bites, stings and scrapes.

Comfrey has been used for centuries, and anyone with a broken bone not only drank comfrey tea and used warmed leaves as a poultice wrapped over the area, but ate it cooked like spinach or in a broth with celery and carrots.

No garden should ever be without comfrey as it is a superb natural fertiliser. Dogs with arthritis will eat the leaves and benefit from having comfrey tea in their drinking water and chopped up in their food, and so will the cats with urinary infections, and so will the chickens to keep them fit.

Comfrey is really incredible!

CAUTION: It is advisable not to take comfrey tea internally. Only ever do so with your doctor's consent.External application of comfrey is safe.

ECHINACEA

Echinacea purpurea, E. angustifolia

Echinacea is the buzzword on boosting the immune system and it is one of the most extraordinary healing herbs. It's been around for centuries, first used by the American Indians—it is a beautiful prairie plant, native to America, and modern research only verifies what the American Indians knew centuries ago.

It has exceptional anti-inflammatory action, it is a natural antibiotic, it is anti-allergenic, and it detoxifies, heals wounds and stimulates the immune system to inhibit the ability of viruses and bacteria to invade cells, and it literally activates the defence system.

Modern medicine uses echinacea to treat allergies, fever blisters and asthma, specially in children. It is also useful for treating fungal infections, rabies and even chilblains, as it prevents them from bursting and allowing infection to set in.

A tea can be made by adding 1 cup of boiling water to 1/4 cup of fresh leaves, flowers and root. Leave to stand for five minutes, then strain. This tea can be sipped for all the above ailments as well as for sore throats, mouth ulcers, flu, coughs, colds, pneumonia, bronchitis and streaming nose and sinusitis. Two to three cups can be taken daily during the infection and once it has cleared up stop, do not use it continuously. Take the tea at the first sign of infection, and continue for up to ten to fourteen days, then stop.

Echinacea dies down during the winter, so it can be dried for the winter—use slightly less than 1/4 cup of dried material. Store in an airtight jar. Cooled tea is an effective wound dressing—apply frequently. Use a spritz bottle to spray it onto the area. The American Indians even used the stalks as a splint packed along a broken limb and soaked in the tea!

COMFREY ARTHRITIS TEA

Take 1 cup only twice a week with your doctor's consent.

¼ cup of fresh comfrey leaves
¼ cup of lucerne sprigs
3 crushed cardamom pods
2 teaspoons of apple cider vinegar

Take comfrey leaves and lucerne sprigs. Pour 2 cups of boiling water over the herbs and add cardamom pods. Stand for 5 minutes. Strain. Add apple cider vinegar and sip while warm. Save the second cup in the fridge, covered, for 2 days later.

Comfrey (left) and Lucerne (right)
work well together in this tea.

IMMUNE-BOOSTING ECHINACEA

¼ cup of echinacea leaves, flowers and root
¼ cup of elderberries
2 sprigs of thyme
juice of one lemon
½ teaspoon of cayenne pepper

Take echinacea leaves, flowers and root,
elderberries and thyme. Cover with 4 cups of boiling
water and simmer for 4 minutes. Cool. Strain. Add
lemon juice and cayenne pepper. Drink ½ a cup
at 2–3 hourly intervals through the day for treating
flu and bronchitis. Then stop. Only take this tea at
the start of, and during, the actual illness—not as a
general tea.

ELDERFLOWER

Sambucus nigra

An ancient, loved, revered and respected small shrubby tree, the elder has been called the 'medicine chest tree' in Europe and Asia where it is indigenous, and has been used since the earliest centuries.

Every part of the tree has been used for all sorts of things—the ripe berries for wine and jam and cough mixtures; the flowers for teas and champagne and cosmetics; the leaves for insect repelling mixtures (which it must be noted are poisonous); and even the hollow branches can be turned into flutes and pea shooters!

But it is the flowers that are so exquisite in a summer, honey-sweet nectar tea!

Pick off the sprays of tiny white flowers that look like lace and discard the thicker stems. You will need 1 tablespoon of fresh flowers for 1 cup of boiling water. Stir and stand for three to five minutes, then add a teaspoon of honey and a squeeze of fresh lemon juice. Sip it slowly.

Elderflowers make remarkable skin treatments. So this tea will help to clear skin problems, refine enlarged pores, remove oiliness and if used as a spray lotion—the cooled tea without the honey—will act as a superb skin cleanser and softener.

One cup of elderflower tea in the morning and one in the afternoon will help to reduce fever, ease a cough and a sore throat, reduce catarrh, hay fever and ear infections, and our grandmothers grew elder trees in their gardens, which they used for not only health, but beauty care too.

One of the most important new research programmes has found that elderflowers with equal quantities of peppermint sprigs (Mentha piperita nigra) made into a tea as above and a cup taken daily, will help to clear the herpes simplex virus from the body (the one that causes fever blisters).

Fennel

Foeniculum vulgare

The slimmer's herb, fennel is one of the most marvellous diuretics, and all parts of this easy and prolific plant can be used! It is a fantastic detoxifier, digestive and cleansing herb, and no one should ever be without it!

Its pleasant licorice-like flavour gives the tea such a delicious quality that everyone loves–even teenage boys with acne will happily drink it!

Make the tea by twisting a portion of its fine feathery leaf into the cup–crush it while doing so to quickly release its wonderful sap. You need ¼ cup, or even 1/3 cup, then pour over boiling water and leave it to stand for five minutes. Strain and drink it down unsweetened.

The tea will ease digestive upsets, heartburn, colic, sour belchings and flatulence, and will settle cramps and distensions and bloatings. It will ease even kidney stones and is a mild expectorant and makes an excellent gargle for sore throats.

For breastfeeding mums, this tea will aid milk production and thus ease baby's digestion and even colic, and for morning sickness, with a squeeze of lemon, fennel tea is superb.

Fennel tea is great as an all-round cleanser, it helps relieve fluid retention, and after too much partying and over imbibing and over eating, two or three cups of fennel tea next day with only fresh fruit to eat, will help to flush the kidneys and put things right again.

There are three kinds of fennel to grow, and all work the same way: the very easy, common all-year-round fennel–leaves, flowers and stems included: Foeniculum vulgare. Then there is the beautiful bronze fennel–the same thing but dark maroon in colour. And then there is Foeniculum dulce–the one that forms the big fleshy bulb which you can shave into the tea as well.

ELDERFLOWER BEAUTY

½ cup of fresh elderflowers, stalks discarded,

2 teaspoons of grated lemon zest

juice of 1 lemon

½ cup of dried calendula flowers

Take elderflowers, lemon zest and juice and calendula flowers. Simmer for 10 minutes in 4 cups of water. Cool and strain. Drink ½ a cup daily, warmed, and use the cooled tea as a lotion.

Fennel Slimmers Tea

¼ cup of fresh fennel leaf

2 teaspoons of fennel seed

¼ cup of fresh basil leaves

Pour 1 cup of boiling water over fresh fennel leaf and fennel seed. Stir and allow to draw. After 5 minutes strain, add apple cider vinegar and stir well. Do not be tempted to sweeten. Take 1–2 cups daily for 10 days, stop for 4 days, then continue. This tea is excellent with fresh basil leaves as a detoxifier after wrong eating.

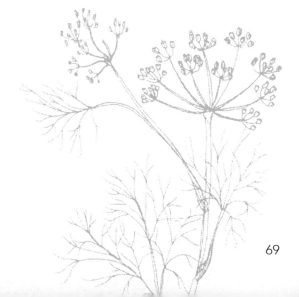

GINGER

Zingiber officinale

Ginger is one of the world's best medicines, and one of the most delicious of all the herb teas. A few thin slices of fresh ginger root—enough to fill 1/4 of a cup—with 1 cup of boiling water poured over it, and gently mashed, with a teaspoon of honey, will act so much like a warming, de-stressing, comforting, refreshing elixir that you'll easily become addicted!

Ginger tea aids the circulation and thus soothes chilblains, and it has anti-inflammatory and antiseptic qualities. Ginger tea settles nausea, stomach aches, flatulence, gripey colic, knocks colds and flu on the head, warms, revitalises, soothes a fever and a throbbing headache, and eases aching muscles and that chilled to the bone feeling, and will generally help to make you feel good all over.

I am never without a root or two in my fridge, and have found that a cup of ginger tea and honey first thing in the morning warms and settles the stomach, specially if there is a taxing or anxiety-filled day ahead. And at the end of that frantic day I don't switch on the percolator, I switch on the kettle for ginger tea which literally smoothes all the troubles away.

Growing your own ginger is fun as well. Just tuck a piece or two of the rhizome that has an 'eye' on it into well-dug, well-composted soil in full sun and watch it grow. When the leaves and pretty scented edible flowers fade and die down your root will be ready to carefully dig up. Wash it well and leave it to stand for two weeks before using it. It matures to its fabulous flavour during that time.

Ginger is the world's favourite spice!

GOLDENROD

Solidago species

Native to Europe and Asia and now naturalised in North America, this showy herbaceous perennial is one of the antique flowers so loved in medieval times, when the monks made medicine, and wine, from its brilliantly yellow autumn plumes.

Pick a few sprays, enough to fill just over 1/4 of a cup, top up with boiling water and let it stand for five minutes. Strain and sip slowly. It is pleasant enough without sweetening, so enjoy it plain.

Since I realised how soothing a tea goldenrod is, and I experienced how quickly and gently and yet effectively it eases hot flushes and cystitis and any bladder infection, I have always made sure I have a patch or two growing nearby.

Now new research has found that goldenrod can fight against the Candida fungus, the cause of oral and vaginal thrush, and it is a superb and gentle treatment for chronic nasal catarrh, postnasal drip, gastro-enteritis and urinary tract infections, even chronic urinary tract infections.

Goldenrod has anti-inflammatory, diuretic and astringent properties which are helpful in treating arthritis and gout, and the back pain associated with kidney ailments.

The slightly cooled tea can be used soaked in a cloth as a poultice over wounds and aching joints, and also added to the bath or used as a wash and lotion for thrush.

Our grandmothers used goldenrod to treat diarrhoea, sore throats and coughs, and to ease menstrual pains and allergic rhinitis, and I have to agree with what herbalist John Gerard wrote in 1597: 'Goldenrod is extolled over all other herbs.' It is an amazing herb and we don't use it enough in these rushed days that engulf us.

GINGER COLD CURE

¼ cup of thinly sliced fresh ginger root
2 teaspoons of lemon rind thinly pared
½ tablespoon of lemon juice
2 teaspoons of honey
¼ teaspoon of cayenne pepper

Take ginger, lemon rind and juice, honey, cayenne pepper and 1 cup of boiling water. Pour the boiling water over the ginger and crush it with a teaspoon. Add all the other ingredients and stir well. The cayenne pepper is a fabulous 'antiseptic' for the throat. Sip slowly. Take 3 cups of this brew hot through the day until the cold eases—usually 2 days.

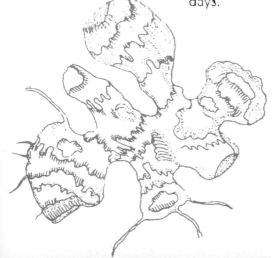

Goldenrod
Anti-inflammatory Tea

¼ cup of fresh or dried goldenrod flowers

¼ cup of lucerne sprigs,

3 slices of ginger root

juice of ½ lemon

honey to sweeten

Take goldenrod flowers and a few leaves. Pour over this 1½ cups of boiling water. Add lucerne sprigs and ginger. Stand for 5 minutes, strain, then add the lemon juice, sweetened with honey if liked, and drink ½ cup warmed, 3 times during the day.

GREEN TEA

Camellia sinensis

Tea is the world's most popular beverage, and yet no one thinks of tea in its many forms as a herb, even though it has been used in Chinese medicine for 5 000 years!

It was in the 1970s that scientists became aware that people who drank green tea had greater protection against strokes, cancer, high cholesterol, high blood pressure, heart attacks and infections—in particular, respiratory and urinary infections.

Green tea's powerfully antioxidant phenols boost the immune system and ease chronic coughs, colds and sore throats, and repair cell damage that occurs in the beginning stages of heart disease, cataracts, macular degeneration and other degenerative conditions like cancer.

Green tea has anti-tumour properties as well as antibacterial, diuretic and astringent properties, and even rinsing and gargling with green tea will help to clear mouth infections and slow down decay of the teeth and other dental problems.

Cooled tea makes a wonderful beauty aid, and a big pot added to the bath softens the skin and eases tension.

I like to drink my green tea like the old Chinese Emperor did over 5 000 years ago—dried straight from the bush—not rolled or sweated or processed, just plain dried.

To make the tea, use 1/4 cup dried leaves to 1 cup boiling water, stand for five minutes, strain, sweeten with honey and add a squeeze of lemon juice if liked. Don't discard the leaves—save them for the next and the next cup—they're full of goodness. Drink up!

JASMINE

Jasminum species

Jasmine is exquisitely fragrant and one of the world's most treasured garden plants. The genus of about 200 species of jasmine is a glorious collection of this ancient plant that has been used through the centuries to make a calming, soothing and unwinding tea, often added to ordinary teas for its therapeutic effect.

It is the fresh flowers that are used (and not the leaves) in the scenting and flavouring of both China and Indian teas, and they make a rare and beautiful tea on their own.

Several species of jasmine have a long history in perfumery, and jasmine essential oil is amongst the most expensive of the essential oils. Jasmine officinalis and J. grandiflorum are used for oil extraction.

Jasminum sambac or Arabian jasmine is a beautiful sprawling shrubby semi-climber or scrambler with clusters of flowers all through the year, and these flowers are particularly wonderful for scenting green tea which is taken for ear and eye infections and to lower blood pressure in South East Asia where it is grown commercially.

Now recently Jasmine officinalis has become available for the first time to South Africa, after my seven-year trials at the Herbal Centre which has made me quite ecstatic. Use 6 flowers (it flowers all year round in sprays that are quite sparse, unlike our spring special, Jasminum polyanthemum) to 1 cup of boiling water, leave to stand for three minutes, then add a squeeze of lemon juice and sip slowly and chew the flowers to really taste the precious oil.

Add fresh flowers to your favourite tea and keep the tin sealed. Take for depression, tension, anxiety and indigestion.

CAUTION: Avoid during pregnancy!

GREEN TEA TONIC

Green tea is so important as a tonic–we should have 1 cup daily if possible. This is my favourite way of making green tea.

CAUTION: Green tea also contains caffeine, so those with irregular heart beat or pregnant mothers or those with stomach ulcers should not take more than one to two cups a day as its high level of alkaloids can, to some extent, increase the heart rate.

¼ cup of green tea leaves
a sliver of lemon rind.
1 tablespoon of lemon juice
1 teaspoon of honey

Take green tea leaves or 1 tea bag. Pour over this 1 cup of boiling water. Add lemon rind. Let it draw for 6 or 7 minutes. Strain. Add lemon juice, honey and sip slowly. I am mad about this tea and highly recommend it.

AUTHENTIC JASMINE TEA

This is the old-fashioned Chinese way to make jasmine tea.

seveal bunches of jasmine flowers
one tea bag of green tea
3 cloves
juice of ½ lemon
grated lemon zest
1 teaspoon honey

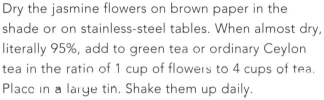

Dry the jasmine flowers on brown paper in the shade or on stainless-steel tables. When almost dry, literally 95%, add to green tea or ordinary Ceylon tea in the ratio of 1 cup of flowers to 4 cups of tea. Place in a large tin. Shake them up daily.

Now add ¼ cup of flowers and green tea to 1 cup of boiling water with cloves. Stand for 3–5 minutes, stir often. Strain. Add lemon juice, a little grated lemon zest and honey. Stir well. Sip slowly.

Avoid during pregnancy.

LAVENDER

Lavandula intermedia (either Grosso or Margaret Roberts lavender)

Of all the hundreds of lavenders it is only the Lavandula intermedia species in the Southern Hemisphere, or the Lavandula angustifolia species in the Northern Hemisphere, that makes a good, palatable and wonderfully soothing and unwinding tea.

(The Lavandula intermedia var. Margaret Roberts used to be known as L. angustifolia Herbal Centre Giant as it originated in the Herbal Centre gardens and it has the typical English lavender look. Now, with the help of overseas growers, it has been found to be a species of L. intermedia and it is infinitely suitable for growing in the Southern Hemisphere, which is way too hot for L. angustifolia species. So remember its parents are species of L. angustifolia and L. latifolia, which makes it the best edible–or in this case drinkable–lavender.)

This exquisite lavender relaxes, calms, soothes, de-stresses, eases muscle tension and muscle spasms, and is a superb antidepressant and has antiseptic, antibacterial and antifungal properties. It stimulates the blood flow and has extremely low toxicity–so it can be used lavishly.

A cup of lavender tea will have the most comforting, calming and unwinding effect after a frantic day. It will help you sleep, ease that throbbing head and smooth away the frown and worry lines.

It eases wind, indigestion and anxiety, and it calms those wild and fast worrying thoughts. I make a big pot of lavender tea, pour off a cup and add the rest, flowers and all, to my bath, and I add a few drops of pure lavender essential oil, and scrub away the cares with lavender soap while I sip my tea! It's a lifesaver!

LEMON

Citrus limon, C. hystrix

Who would have thought the lowly lemon is a herb? It is! And one of the most precious of all herbs! It is the juice, the peel, the blossom and, in the case of the fascinating Caffea lime (Citrus hystrix), the leaves!

All parts of this can't-do-without fruit contain natural alkalisers and natural astringents. It also has natural inflammatory properties, it acts as a blood cleanser, a nerve tonic, a diuretic, and it contains chemicals that help to block cancer, fight respiratory ailments and clear toxins.

The high vitamin content in the lemon enhances its antibacterial and antiviral properties, and the anti-oxidant bounty it contains in the skin has a profoundly beneficial effect on the human body. It literally is a health builder and it also helps to lower high blood pressure and high blood cholesterol. We should be eating a lemon a day!

The Spaniards were as passionate about lemons as the Italians, and both have ancient medical texts showing how important the juice, as well as the skin and pith, were to build health when medication was so simple. This fascinating information shows that fresh lemon zest was preserved in vinegar for times when there was no fruit, and so treasured special clay vats and flasks were made for it. Thinly pared rind was boiled in water for coughs and sore throats and lung ailments, and crushed with other herbs like rosemary and sage—centuries ago.

The lemons we know today are so different to those ancient lemons after hybridisation and cross-pollination—just hold a lemon in your hand and think back on its amazing journey to the tree that grows in your garden today.

A tea can be made of thin parings of the rind and three slices of lemon in one cup of boiling water, stand for three minutes, stir well, strain, sweeten if liked with a touch of honey and sip health—and bless those ancient physicians who taught us about health from lemons!

Relaxing Lavender Tea

2-3 sprigs lavender

3 thin slices of ginger root

1 teaspoon of honey

3 cardamom pods

Take 2–3 sprigs (or enough to fill 1/4 of a cup) of lavender. Pour over this 1 cup of boiling water, add ginger root, honey and cardamom pods. Crush well with a spoon. Stand for 5 minutes, strain and sip slowly, preferably while lying in a bath fragrant with fresh lavender hung under the tap, lavender soap and bath oil and a lavender-scented candle, and relax.

Antioxidant Lemonade

Juice from 12 lemons
2–3 cups of sugar
1 cup of honey
Rind from 2 lemons

Take the lemon juice, sugar, honey, 6 cups of water and lemon rind, finely grated. Mix together and let the sugar dissolve. Add the water and mix well. Chill. Pour into tall glasses with ice cubes and drink as a summer drink, or serve hot in winter as hot lemonade. Wonderful if you have a cold or a sore throat.

LEMON GRASS

Cymbopogon citratus

Lemon grass has to be one of the favourite of all herb teas. Its refreshing, uplifting, invigorating effect puts it into a class of its own, and the remarkable thing is that one never tires of it!

An easy-to-grow perennial, lemon grass needs to be fresh for that wonderful flavour, and in all but the coldest parts of the country it can be picked all through the year. A fresh leaf added to a pot of rooibos tea and served with a slice of fresh lemon and sweetened with honey, refreshes and revives one so reliably after a busy day that even coffee addicts find it acceptable!

The basic lemon grass tea recipe is: one 15 cm long piece of fresh leaf rolled up and bruised and tucked into the cup, covered with 1 cup of boiling water and crushed with a teaspoon until the fragrance is strong enough– usually two to three minutes. Then sweeten with a touch of honey if liked and sip slowly, and the magical brew will immediately take effect. The feeling of relaxation and invigoration at the same time makes one respond so warmly to the tea it will become part of the daily menu.

Lemon grass is an excellent digestive herb, relaxing the muscles of both the stomach and the intestines, so that it relieves colic, cramps, flatulence, colitis and heartburn, and is suitable for children.

For the elderly, lemon grass soothes arthritic aches and pains and acts on the pathogenic flora of the stomach and the bacillus of dysentery and soothes the mucous membranes of the stomach. It helps to bring down fevers and calm stress, tension and anxiety, and aids the circulation as well as deodorising the whole body.

Lemon grass is actually classified as a tonic for all ages–add the cooled tea to fresh fruit juice for a healthy cooldrink!

Lemon Grass Summer Tea

This tea is for the digestion and it's delicious.

2 x 15 cm lengths of fresh lemon grass
1 chilled cup of unsweetened litchi juice or apple juice

Twist the lemon grass into a cup. Add 1 cup of boiling water and let it cool completely. Strain. Add juice. Stir well and serve with ice in a tall glass with a slice of fresh lemon. Beautiful as a cold tea, just before a meal, and as a hot tea to warm you up in mid-winter.

LEMON VERBENA

Lippia citriodora

Lemon verbena is the one herb that still retains its deliciously strong lemony taste when you dry it, and it's all the more deliciously rich if it is freshly picked.

Much loved the world over, lemon verbena is a treasured shrub in every hothouse and is lovingly tended for its incredibly flavour-filled leaves.

Lemon verbena has a pronounced tonic effect on the nervous system, which gives it the status of being an excellent de-stressing herb and a natural antidepressant.

Medical research has found it excellent for treating nervous upsets, palpitations, headaches, colds, bronchitis, congestion, cramps, nausea and even heartache. It will aid the circulation, comfortingly aid the digestion, it is a remarkable expectorant and will settle an over-active wound-up child.

Lemon verbena grows well in a large tub as well as in the open ground, and it needs full sun and a good twice-yearly barrow of rich compost. It is deciduous and benefits from light winter pruning and tidying up, and it will reward you with years of fragrant leaves.

Pour 1 cup of boiling water over 10 lemon verbena leaves (enough to fill ¼ of a cup), leave it to stand for five minutes, then strain, stir into it a touch of honey if liked and sip slowly.

Children love it cooled and add to fresh fruit juices. For nausea and cramps add three or four thin slices of ginger root and a squeeze of lemon juice and sip slowly.

Dry the leaves on newspaper in the shade at the end of summer and store in a glass screw-top jar for winter use. Use 6 or 7 dried leaves to 1 cup of boiling water and stand for five minutes before straining. Sweeten with honey and add a slice of fresh lemon for a winter tea.

Lemon Verbena Tea

This tea is equally good for upsets, depression and headaches as for colds and congestion—it really makes you feel better.

¼ cup of fresh lemon verbena leaves

3 slices of ginger

1 fresh lemon leaf

a touch of honey

Take fresh lemon verbena leaves, pour over this 1 cup of boiling water, add ginger and fresh lemon leaf. Stand for 4 minutes, then strain and sip slowly. Add a touch of honey if liked. It is delicious cold with ice as well and with pineapple juice added. (

If you are growing Citrus hysterix, the kaffir lime, use a leaf of it. It's delicious, otherwise a leaf from any lemon tree will do.

LEMON MYRTLE AND MANUKA HONEY TEA

This tea is called 'the singers brew'. Combined with the antibacterial qualities of manuka honey, lemon myrtle leaves (Backhousia citriodora) soothe sore throats and help with winter colds.

4 fresh lemon myrtle leaves or dried lemon myrtle

or 1 teaspoon dried lemon myrtle

1 teaspoon manuka honey

Place the leaves and honey in a cup. Add 1 cup of boiling water. Stir and sip slowly. You can also add fresh slices of ginger for extra punch.

LEMON THYME

Thymus vulgaris citriodorus

All varieties of thyme have antiseptic, antibacterial and antifungal properties and all are rich in precious health-boosting oils. Thymus citriodorus is particularly delicious with its strong lemony scent. Use ¼ cup of fresh sprigs in 1 cup of boiling water, stand for three to five minutes then strain, add a squeeze of lemon juice and one slice of lemon and sip slowly. This precious tea will be soothing for sore throats, coughs, colds, allergic rhinitis, hayfever, aches and pains (even backache, as it relaxes tense muscles), asthma, bronchitis and insomnia. In fact, a tub of lemon thyme growing prettily at the back door in full sun will become so important for the herb tea lover that it will be nurtured, watered and composted often to have an abundant supply of deliciousness.

Interestingly, all the thymes have been found to have marvellous expectorant qualities and so, added to ginger, lemon, sage and honey in a tea, you have a formula for an extraordinarily effective cough mixture: 4 thin slices of fresh ginger root, juice of half a lemon, 1 teaspoon of grated lemon rind, 1 tablespoon of fresh roughly chopped sage leaves and 1 tablespoon fresh lemon thyme sprigs, pour over this 1 mug of boiling water and stir and bruise with a teaspoon. Add honey to taste, usually 2 teaspoons, stir well, then sip slowly (not all at once, but every now and then) keeping it warm in a tea cosy or styrofoam cooler box.

Lemon thyme has the ability to stimulate the body's production of white blood corpuscles to resist infection and is claimed to be an anti-ageing herb!

Use the cooled tea with lots of freshly squeezed lemon juice and honey to make a lemon thyme lemonade–served with crushed ice on a summer's day, it's a stunner!

LINSEED

Flax Linum usitatissimum

One of the world's oldest known plants, linseed or flax has been enjoyed and respected for centuries as a health giver. New research is proving it to be so beneficial that it should be growing everywhere! It is so easy, so pretty, so reapable and so rewarding you'll quickly wonder why linseed hasn't been a feature in your garden!

Sow the seed in shallow furrows in well-dug, well-composted soil in full sun in spring through to autumn at intervals of three weeks. In this way you'll always have a pickable crop.

The flowers, exquisite, blue and dainty, are edible and make a delicious tea and the sprays of encapsulated seeds, reaped when light brown and dry, can be stored and used throughout the year. Give the seeds a few crushes in a big pestle and mortar to break the shiny brown case on each tiny seed.

Use 1 tablespoon of the flowers and leafy sprigs–or 'little bits of sky' as my grandmother called them–pour over this 1 cup of boiling water, stand for three minutes, then strain, add lemon juice and a touch of honey if liked. Or take 2 teaspoons of seeds (you can buy these at the health shops), crush lightly and add 1 cup of boiling water, stand for five minutes and stir well. Sip slowly, chew the seeds too.

Linseed tea is the most beautifully soothing tea for the digestive tract. It will ease constipation, soothe irritation and heartburn and colic and flatulence in the digestive tract and, because it is so rich in mucilage and unsaturated fats, it will soothe chest ailments and bronchial and respiratory problems, and bladder and kidney ailments, as well as arthritic pains. The oil that is contained in the precious little shiny seeds is a hugely important source of essential fatty acids which help to reduce the build-up of fatty deposits in the cells and will ease chronic urinary and respiratory conditions.

This is one of our essential future health boosters–get that row in now– don't delay!

LEMON THYME TEA

This anti-aging tea is stunning! And it eases that backache and stiff shoulders!

¼ cup of lemon thyme sprigs

1 cup of green melon pieces

1 cup of green grape juice

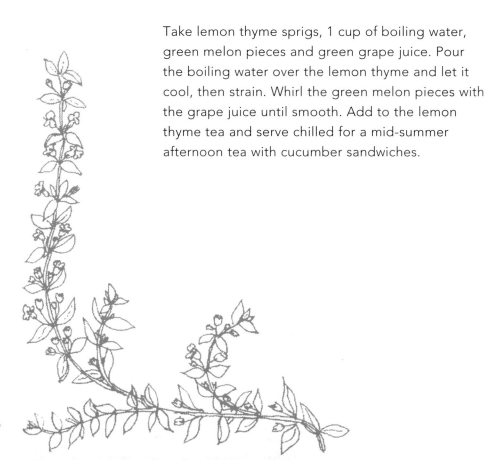

Take lemon thyme sprigs, 1 cup of boiling water, green melon pieces and green grape juice. Pour the boiling water over the lemon thyme and let it cool, then strain. Whirl the green melon pieces with the grape juice until smooth. Add to the lemon thyme tea and serve chilled for a mid-summer afternoon tea with cucumber sandwiches.

Linseed Tea for Chest Ailments

Don't forget this precious plant is also good for bladder and kidney ailments and arthritic pains. This tea is fabulous.

½ cup of crushed and pounded linseeds
2 tablespoons of lindseed flowers, buds and leafy sprigs
1 thumb-length sprig of peppermint
2 slices of lemon
the juice of ½ a lemon
2 teaspoons of thinly pared lemon rind
2 teaspoons of honey

Combine linseeds, flowers, buds and leafy sprigs, peppermint, lemon and juice and lemon rind, honey and 1 cup of boiling water. Stand for 5–8 minutes, then strain. Take 2 cups a day for bladder ailments, or 1 cup daily for anything else.

LUCERNE

Alfalfa Medicago sativa

I am quite thrilled with lucerne–in fact I am almost lyrical about it! Did you know that half a cup of fresh lucerne sprigs and flowers in your daily salad will give you such a boost of minerals, vitamins and energy you'll run all day and want to dance all night?

A cup of fresh lucerne tea–its nutrients so easily assimilated it literally gives you a burst of vitality–will lift your heart, raise your flagging spirits and soothe your worried anxious thoughts so effectively, you'll be enthralled: ¼ cup fresh leaves and flowers, pour over this 1 cup of boiling water, stand for five minutes, strain.

Interestingly, lucerne tea and fresh lucerne leaves in the diet are being researched at present as a treatment for alcohol and drug abuse. Already research has verified lucerne's excellence in treating menstrual problems, menopause discomfort, particularly hot flushes, hot sweats and heart palpitations during menopause, as it has superb oestrogenic activity. It also contributes to the building up of body strength, energy and vitality–it literally acts like a tonic. The high content of vitamins A, D, E, G and K and iron boost energy levels quickly, and students during exam times find lucerne tablets (available from health shops and chemists) invaluable.

Arthritic pains are eased and soothed by lucerne tea and alfalfa sprouts eaten in the daily salad, and a particularly potent energiser, very useful after a debilitating illness, and a pain-relieving tea, can be made by pouring 1 cup of boiling water over ¼ cup fresh lucerne sprigs and flowers and 1 tablespoon of fresh alfalfa sprouts. Stand for three to five minutes, then strain and sip slowly.

Any lucerne tea left over can be cooled and watered into an ailing plant. It will quickly revive it and promote new growth.

CAUTION: Doctors suggest that those suffering from auto-immune diseases should not take lucerne frequently.

MAIDENHAIR FERN

Adiantum capillus-veneris

Who would have thought this exquisite pot plant, so loved for centuries in every conservatory and on every shady verandah, could be made into a tea?

Sip slowly to ease coughs, colds, asthma, shortness of breath, catarrh, runny nose, sore throats, chronic postnasal drip, bronchitis and exhaustion. The Zulu people take the tea for measles and chicken pox too!

It is a gently soothing tea that can also be served cold with the addition of fresh lemon juice and boiled with soft brown sugar to make that ancient and much loved drink of the courts, 'capillaire'. If the brown sugar is replaced with honey and a dash of brandy is added, maidenhair tea makes an excellent night-time 'hot toddy' for a cough and a cold and a sore throat.

On a hot summer's day, chill the maidenhair tea and add equal quantities of either white grape juice or litchi juice and serve it with crushed ice as a party drink. For a cold winter night, drink warm cups of maidenhair fern tea at the fireside and add a dash or two or three of hot bottled cherries that have been stoned and whirled in their syrup in a liquidiser to a thick luscious sweetener with a little brandy, and watch your guests' delighted surprise specially when this treat is served hot after dinner just before they leave for home. This delicious 'toddy' will chase away any chills

Always use the mature fronds of the maidenhair for the teas as the mature leaves contain the soothing gel-like mucilage which is released during boiling. The monks in ancient days boiled maidenhair fern with honey for a day and dispensed it hot mixed with wine for coughs, colds and flu to the suffering villagers, who called it 'hottod'. Is that perhaps where 'hot toddy' comes from?

LUCERNE ENERGY BOOST

¼ cup of fresh lucerne sprigs with flowers
1 sprig of sacred basil with about 4 leaves on it
honey and lemon juice

Take lucerne sprigs and basil and pour over this 1 cup of boiling water. Crush a little and stir well with the spoon. Sweeten with a little honey if liked, and/ or add a little fresh lemon juice and a little bit of lemon zest. Strain. Sip slowly. This tea will wake you up and get you running smoothly!

MAIDENHAIR TEA

¼ cup of maidenhair fern fronds

thumb-length sprigs of lemon thyme

1 slice of lemon

juice of 1/2 lemon

honey to sweeten

Take mature maidenhair fern fronds and lemon thyme. Pour over 1 cup of boiling water and crush gently for 2 minutes. Strain after 5 minutes. Sweeten with honey and add a slice of lemon and squeeze in the juice. Sip slowly—it's delicious and soothes the throat.

Marjoram

Origanum majorana

This much-loved culinary herb is a powerhouse of soothing, calming and healing properties.

Carried during the Middle Ages as a protective charm, it has been used through the centuries to treat bruising, to settle nausea, colic, flatulence and bloating of the stomach, to calm an anxious child and, with catnip, to ease bed-wetting problems, and to clear mucous from throat and nose, to ease coughs, colds, tonsillitis and even pleurisy.

It is a natural antispasmodic so it immediately calms, quietens and soothes, and as a tea at the end of a stress-filled, anxious day, marjoram is simply marvellous. Recent medical research verifies marjoram's antiseptic, antibacterial and antispasmodic properties and finds that it combines well with ginger, lemon balm and thyme as a treatment for aching joints, backache and respiratory and digestive ailments.

Taken as a tea–¼ cup fresh sprigs to 1 cup of boiling water, leave to stand for five minutes, then strain and sip slowly–marjoram will quickly go to work. Add a squeeze of lemon juice for coughs and colds. Combine 2 thumb-length sprigs of marjoram with 2 thumb-length sprigs of catmint in ½ cup of boiling water, leave to stand for five minutes, then give ¼ cup to an anxious child just before going to bed. It will ease nightmares, bed-wetting and restlessness.

Marjoram is an ancient symbol of happiness, and once you have quietly sipped a cup of marjoram tea you will realise what a wonderful little 'happy-making' herb this is–it really calms, soothes and lifts the spirits.

New research is looking into marjoram and its close cousin oreganum as a treatment for panic attacks and arthritic and rheumatic aches and pains.

Marjoram Tea

Wonderfully comforting, this tea soothes aching legs, back and neck, muscles and heartburn and helps you sleep.

¼ cup of marjoram sprigs
¼ cup of lemon balm (melissa) sprigs
4 thin slices of fresh ginger root
a good squeeze of lemon juice
2 teaspoons honey
4 cloves
4 basil leaves

Pour 2 cups of boiling water over the marjoram sprigs and lemon balm sprigs. Add fresh ginger root, a good squeeze of lemon juice, honey, cloves and basil leaves and stir well, crushing thoroughly. Stand for 5 minutes. Strain. Sip ½ a cup of hot tea four times through the day—the last cup just before you go to bed. You'll sleep easily.

Melissa (lemon balm)

Melissa officinalis

Over 2 000 years ago lemon balm was an important medicine for the digestion, for fear and anxiety and for insomnia, amongst a thousand other treatments, and modern medical research has substantiated these ancient virtues of this precious, easy-to-grow perennial herb.

Lemon balm or lemon mint or melissa, as it is commonly known, is truly one of the most marvellous digestive herbs ever known, and it is as loved and respected throughout the world today as it was centuries ago.

No one can afford not to know and grow lemon balm, for the list of ailments it effectively treats affects us all at some time or another. Lemon balm is a calming, soothing, destressing, unwinding herb, good for all age groups and is one of the most wonderful treatments for hyperactive, excitable, noisy, difficult children. Lemon balm tea is made by pouring 1 cup of boiling water over ¼ cup of fresh lemon balm sprigs (and only use fresh—dry leaves have no taste and are devoid of the important actions that make lemon balm so effective), leave to stand for five minutes, then strain and sip slowly. Its fresh lemony taste makes it delicious and the cooled tea can be added to fresh unsweetened fruit juice—a superb cooldrink that children love.

A cup or two of lemon balm tea daily will aid circulation, help to lower high blood pressure, ease heartburn, colic, nausea, bloating, sour belching, flatulence, spastic colon, cramps, painful menstruation, diverticulitis, flu—with muscular aches and pains—anxiety, depression, sleeplessness, irritability, despair, headaches, nervousness, chicken pox, shingles, acne, greasy spotty skin. Cooled tea added to the bath, will help to relax and ease tension out of necks, backs and aching legs. It is also safe for babies—a teaspoon or two of cooled lemon balm tea will save many a situation and can be given often.

Once you try it, you'll become a lemon balm lover—like me!

MELISSA AND OATS

I love this precious tea—it diffuses all the anxiety and tension like nothing else, and I store my ripened oats in a jar for quick teas all year round.

¼ cup of lemon balm sprigs
¼ cup of ripened oats, either fresh or dry, still in their husks

Pour 1 cup of boiling water over lemon balm sprigs and ripened oats. Crush well and stand for 5 minutes. Strain and sweeten if liked with honey —but its minty, lemony taste is so pleasant you'll probably not need the honey. Strain, sip slowly and feel the tension disappear after three sips!

Oats in their husks

MINT

Mentha species

Mint is a much-loved, much-used and much-respected herb all over the world that has been around for centuries. Vials and urns filled with dried mint have been found in sacred burial sites in the pyramids and in temples dating back to before 1000 BC.

It was the Romans who spread mint through Europe, and on into Britain and from there to the rest of the world where it flourishes today as loved and cherished as it was so long ago.

There are numerous varieties and all have the same key actions: antispasmodic, digestive, antiseptic and analgesic. It increases sweating and so helps to detoxify the body and cleanse the liver, and all the varieties stimulate the secretion of bile.

A mint tea is the most delicious way to ease heartburn, flatulence, colic, nausea, feverish conditions and even headaches and migraines. For example peppermint, Mentha piperita nigra, will soothe, calm and quieten exam-time nerves, yet it will help you stay alert with a clear mind and retain facts, and spearmint, Mentha longifolia polyadena, will help to ease tension, digest very spicy and very rich food, and is beautifully cleansing if the cooled tea is added to the bath.

A cup of mint tea can be made by pouring 1 cup of boiling water over ¼ cup fresh sprigs of any of the mints, letting it stand for five minutes, then strain, sweeten with honey if liked or add a pinch of cinnamon powder to chocolate mint tea (Mentha spicata var. piperita) or add lemon juice and sip slowly to let it do its digestive work, and the world's worries literally recede.

Mint is so easy to grow, we should all have at least three of the wonderful varieties in our garden to fully enjoy the benefits of mint. It is a voracious feeder, so be sure to give it lots of compost, and it loves moisture and it can take a little shade.

Mint Digestive Tea

Everyone loves mint and I serve this fabulous digestive at the end of a party!

Pour 2 cups of boiling water over ¼ cup of fresh sprigs of your favourite mint, ¼ cup of fresh lemon balm sprigs, 1 teaspoon of caraway seeds and 1 teaspoon of fennel seeds. Crush and stir well. Stand for 5 minutes, then strain out the sprigs but leave the seeds in. Sip ½ a cup slowly after dinner and ½–¾ cup before going to bed and chew the seeds. Or, for chronic heartburn, sip ¼ cup 3 or 4 times through the day.

NUTMEG

Myristica fragrans

There really is something quite compelling about freshly grated nutmeg. It's warming, comforting, delicious, charming, fragrant, and sprinkled onto hot milk or into a cup of hot water, it enfolds one in warmth and comfort and a nurtured feeling of wellbeing.

This precious tropical plant has been cherished for centuries. Its nuts in their cases of mace have been used through the centuries throughout the tropics for easing the digestion, reducing heartburn, nausea, bloating, colic and flatulence. Just less than 1 teaspoon of freshly grated nutmeg in 1 cup of boiling water has been used through the centuries in China, in Sri Lanka and in Hawaii as a treatment for diarrhoea and stomach upsets, rheumatism and muscular aches and pains, and indigestion.

Our grandmothers took nutmeg tea for skin problems and spots and greasiness—less than 1 teaspoon freshly grated into 1 cup of boiling water was sipped with a squeeze of lemon juice once a week. In China, nutmeg tea is taken to increase the appetite.

Medical science does indeed support all these traditional uses and found that nutmeg is a reputable antispasmodic. But it has not yet proved that nutmeg has aphrodisiac properties, as many tribes in the tropics believe!

Low medicinal doses and culinary additions are safe, but always remember nutmeg is potent and too much is toxic. A little goes a long way—don't make it every day.

Buy nutmeg with the mace still attached if ever you can and use the network of mace in cooking—it is exquisitely flavoured. Store whole nutmegs in screw-top jars to keep the freshness in, and grate just enough from a whole nutmeg for your tea.

Nutmeg and Ginger Anti-nausea Tea

This tea will not only soothe the stomach and ease nausea, indigestion and colic, but will ease muscular aches and pains and aching rheumatic joints.

½ teaspoon of freshly grated nutmeg
3 teaspoons of freshly grated ginger
good squeeze of lemon juice

Pound grated nutmeg pounded into grated ginger and stir into 1 cup of boiling water with lemon juice, It's an antispasmodic tea as well. Sip it slowly, as hot as you can enjoy it, and feel the soothing warmth take away the discomfort.

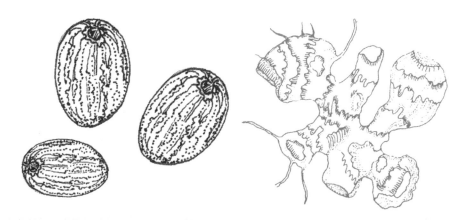

Oat straw

Avena sativa

It is so satisfying growing a row of oats for making tea! It can be grown at any time of the year, although it is best in the cold months, sown in autumn. It was an ancient remedy for rheumatism, and recent research has found that a tea of roughly chopped ripened oat straw is a bone builder, and can help to prevent osteoporosis if taken daily. During medieval times it was taken as a brew to strengthen the body, and particularly the soldiers took it with them on their journeys as a strengthener, and also to ease pain.

The tea, and a gruel of oats, has been used through the centuries to ease arthritic aches and pains, and to prevent bones breaking in the elderly, and to soothe panic and anxiety attacks, and to build resistance. Another marvellous effect oat straw tea has is to strengthen the skin, helping it remain soft, moist and elastic as it ages, and it may help to prevent the thinning of the skin which becomes so fragile in the elderly.

Oats and oat straw contain many important minerals, alkaloids and vitamins, in particular vitamins B1, B2, D and E. Oat straw tea is proving to be helpful in treating degenerative diseases like multiple sclerosis, as well as thyroid deficiency, depression, constantly recurring colds and flu, and slow recovery and lack of energy and vitality. It literally acts as a restorative tonic.

Another marvellous use of oat straw tea is in soothing acne and greasy skin, and for treating menopause it has star status as it assists in reducing oestrogen deficiency.

To make oat straw tea: roughly snip up ¼ cup of oat straw (it must be organically grown and have dried naturally in the field), pour over this 1 cup of boiling water, stand for five minutes then strain.

Oats really is a wonder plant and research now shows that a daily helping of oats porridge (not the instant kind), oat bran and a daily cup or two of oat straw tea can drastically lower high cholesterol. What are we waiting for?

OLIVE LEAF

Olea europaea

The ancient Greeks revered the olive as a symbol of prosperity and achievement, and from the earliest days olive oils were used for both medicine and food. Infused oils, made by the monks in Italy in the early centuries, were used as wound dressings and to treat burns. It is only recent research that has tested olive leaf extract and found it to have some astonishing results.

Extracts of the leaves contain olearopein, a strong antiviral and antibacterial constituent that has the ability to improve the whole circulatory system and to lower the blood sugar levels, which makes it an excellent treatment for diabetes—for which it has been used for centuries.

A tea made of olive leaves has now been found to be an excellent diuretic, and an energising and comforting treatment for chronic fatigue syndrome, for multiple sclerosis, for cystitis, viral attacks—like flu—for high fevers, disorientation, dizziness and feelings of utter despair and helplessness.

A tea of olive leaves taken daily helps to lower high blood pressure, it can increase natural immunity and has now been proven that ME (and chronic fatigue syndrome) responds beautifully to it if taken regularly. For the tea, pour 1 cup of boiling water over ¼ cup fresh olive leaves and sprigs and stand for five minutes. Strain, and add a sprinkle of ground cinnamon, if liked, for an extra taste. Take one to two cups daily for ten days, then give it a break for two to three days, then continue for ten days, break for two to three days, and so on. The cooled tea can be used as a wash for cuts and grazes and scrapes and rashes the way those ancient monks would have done, and added to the bath will soothe itchiness and cool the heat of sunburn.

If you remember that olive trees were first grown in Crete in 3500 BC, isn't it time we re-looked at this remarkable tree?

Oat Straw and Elderflower for Skin Softening

I love this tea! It puts moisture back into the skin and it tastes so blandly refreshing, you actually feel it soothe your mouth!

¼ cup of oats in their husks–just like in the drawing
a few dried oat leaves
¼ cup of dried or fresh elderflowers
1 small piece of cinnamon
Honey to taste

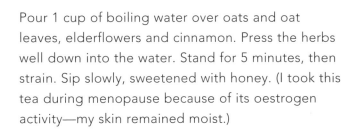

Pour 1 cup of boiling water over oats and oat leaves, elderflowers and cinnamon. Press the herbs well down into the water. Stand for 5 minutes, then strain. Sip slowly, sweetened with honey. (I took this tea during menopause because of its oestrogen activity—my skin remained moist.)

Olive Leaf Energising Tea

This is particularly good for diabetics and for those with chronic fatigue and poor circulation.

¼ cup of fresh olive sprigs
a squeeze of lemon juice or 2 teaspoons of apple cider vinegar

Pour 1 cup of boiling water over olive sprigs and stand for 5 minutes. Strain and add lemon juice or apple cider vinegar. No honey! Stir and sip slowly.

This has got to be a modern-day elixir—simple, quick and so amazingly effective. And olive trees are easy to grow!

Parsley

Petroselinum crispum

One of nature's most amazing plants and used throughout the world from the earliest centuries, parsley is literally a multivitamin in a leaf! A half cup of fresh parsley contains more betacarotene than two large fresh carrots, more vitamin C than two large oranges, 20 times more iron than one serving of liver, and ten times more calcium than one cup of milk!

Eaten by the Romans as a deodoriser and after-orgy breath freshener and refresher, and used by the monks in the Middle Ages to treat everything from hair loss to gout, from chest ailments to bladder infections, parsley has never lost its popularity and has been grown throughout the world as the most popular culinary herb that is recognised everywhere.

Interestingly, parsley has been found to be so effective today for treating gout, rheumatism, arthritis, cystitis, fever, delayed menstruation, nausea, bladder infections, liverishness, prostate problems and for the control of high blood pressure, that medical research continues to verify its ancient uses.

Eating fresh parsley will often bring relief and one to three cups of parsley tea during the day in acute conditions, offer such comfort and ease, it's no wonder parsley is the world's favourite herb!

To make the tea, use ¼ cup fresh sprigs in 1 cup of boiling water, stand for five minutes, strain and sip slowly. As an alkaliser add a slice of lemon to your parsley tea, and as an over-indulgence rectifier add a pinch of cayenne pepper to the parsley tea and the slice of lemon! The Romans had the right idea!

No garden should be without parsley. It is a tonic herb, serve it freshly chopped sprinkled over everything! And it is a marvellous detoxifier, refresher and cleanser.

PINEAPPLE SAGE

Salvia elegans

This is a bright, pretty and easy-to-grow border plant with sprays of delicious red flowers, and the unmistakable and tantalizing scent and taste of pineapple is present in the whole plant.

As a base for teas both hot and iced, this precious plant takes some beating. It's a real party piece and its abundant growth and easy management makes it so worthwhile having in the garden.

To make the tea: ¼ cup of fresh sprigs and flowers to 1 cup of boiling water, stand for five minutes, then strain. Sweeten with honey and add a squeeze of lemon juice and sip slowly to ease a sore throat, to soothe indigestion, and to help calm and unwind and settle down after a frenetic and worrying day.

Pineapple sage is part of the huge salvia or sage family, and it shares some of the properties of the sages, in particular—it also acts like a tonic, renewing spent energy and flagging vitality and that most sought-after feeling of joy in living.

The cooled tea makes a delicious base for a pineapple summer party drink—add equal quantities pineapple juice and cooled pineapple sage tea and add a little crushed, peeled, fresh pineapple and serve chilled, sweetened with honey. Float a sprinkling of the fresh red flowers in the glass—like the leaves they taste of pineapples—and wait for compliments!

As a tough and undemanding perennial, pineapple sage is easy to grow. It benefits from lots of compost dug in around it, full sun and a deep watering twice a week. It needs to be cut back after the flowers are over and new succulent shoots keep emerging, particularly in spring.

For a winter warmer use the leaves in the tea—¼ of a cup—and add a dash of sherry after pouring the boiling water in and standing for two minutes. Sip slowly and feel the chill go.

PINEAPPLE SAGE SUMMER TONIC

¼ cup pineapple sage leaves
1 stick of cinnamon
3 fresh lucerne sprigs
2 slices of fresh pineapple
the pulp of 2 passionfruit

Take pineapple sage leaves. Pour over this 1 cup of boiling water. Add cinnamon and lucerne sprigs and stand for 5 minutes. Strain. Cool. Add fresh pineapple and passionfruit. Whirl in the liquidisor. Serve chilled in a tall glass with lots of ice. Lovely at the end of a long hot day.

Parsley and Celery Detox

This is a simply marvellous detox diuretic for the morning after the night before.

¼ cup of parsley
1/4 cup of celery leaves
a thumb-length sprig of thyme
1 teaspoon of lightly crushed coriander seeds
a slice of lemon

In 1 cup of boiling water add parsley and celery leaves with sprig of thyme, coriander seeds and lemon. It will clear puffy eyes, puffy ankles, hayfever, itchy nose and all those discomforts smoke-filled-noise-filled-over-partying brings. Stand for 5 minutes, strain. Drink slowly with no sweetening. Take a cup 3 times during the day to feel better.

This is a treatment for a hangover from wrong eating too!

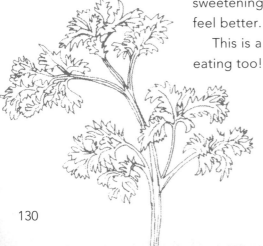

Pennywort

Gotu kola Centella asiatica

This groundcover is an incredible herb. It is amazing in its healing properties and new uses and new research continues to ensure its popularity.

Pennywort is rich in minerals, vitamins, particularly vitamins B and C, glycocides, fatty acids, amino acids and a host of other remarkable properties. It is a superb tonic and no other herb comes near it for its versatility.

Pennywort tea is superb for treating stress, nervousness, anxiety, depression and amnesia, it helps to promote mental calm and clarity and to release tension. It is credited with antiseptic, anti-inflammatory, digestive and diuretic properties, and is used to treat skin ailments from eczema to psoriasis, dermatitis to leprosy, and to speed up the healing process after surgery, and to reduce scar formation – pennywort knows no bounds!

Arthritic pains and swellings, bedsores, poor circulation, urinary tract infections, colds, sore throats, tonsillitis, lupus, peptic ulcers, liver ailments, periodontal diseases, tuberculosis, measles, varicose veins, phlebitis, ulcerative conditions of the legs and venereal diseases, pleurisy, constipation, fibrocytic breasts – all benefit from pennywort.

To make the tea: ¼ cup fresh leaves to 1 cup of boiling water, stand for five minutes, strain and sip slowly – usually a cup to two cups a day for ten days for acute conditions, then give it a break of three to four days, then continue with a cup a day for ten days, break for three to four days, etc. For chronic conditions one cup of pennywort tea on alternate days is the standard dose.

Pennywort is a quick-spreading, easy-to-grow perennial that takes both shade and sun equally well and thrives in compost-enriched fairly moist soil. Grow it!

Pennywort Brain-power Energy Tea

(also known as Tiger's Tea)

Pennywort has got to be one of the world's most versatile herbs and, particularly for its incredible energising and clear-thinking actions, it's nothing short of amazing! Use 3 leaves of pennywort in 1 cup of boiling water with 1 thumb-length sprig of rosemary and 2 sprigs with flowers of lucerne. Crush and stir, then stand for 5 minutes. Add a slice and a squeeze of lemon, sweeten with a touch of honey if liked – I like it plain and strong! Then strain and sip, planning what you'll do and where you'll go first – there will be no stopping you!

RASPBERRY

Rubus indaeus

If you think that the raspberry has been a favourite household remedy for centuries—warriors took raspberry leaves with them on their crusades to wash wounds and to treat soldiers' diarrhoea, and medieval monks used raspberry leaves to heal sore throats, rheumatic pains and eye ailments, and to assist and prepare for child birth—you'll understand why it has been so treasured and so protected a plant all over the world.

Medical science today verifies these ancient treatments, and more besides, and as it is so easy a plant to grow, the raspberry is as popular today as it was in those days of so long ago.

Raspberry leaf tea is pleasant and fresh tasting and, when the berries are ripe, add two or three crushed to the tea for extra taste and goodness. Steep ¼ cup of fresh leaves in 1 cup of boiling water, stand for five minutes, strain and sip slowly. The tea is used to treat indigestion, for mouth ulcers—hold in the mouth before swallowing—for rheumatism, aches and pains, to clear mucous after a cold, to flush kidneys and to ease bladder ailments. A cup of raspberry leaf tea taken only in the last stages of pregnancy is a traditional drink as it is an effective uterine stimulant.

The leaves have astringent properties and the tea makes an excellent mouth wash and gargle for mouth ulcers and gum ailments. The cooled tea can be applied to varicose ulcers and used as a wash and a lotion.

Plant raspberries in well-dug, well-composted soil in full sun and water deeply twice a week. The perennial clump forms and each year old canes need to be cut back to ground level. The fruit is borne on new canes and the plant propagates from new shoots that form at the edges of the clump.

Endlessly interesting, this is a wonderful plant in the garden.

CAUTION: Take the tea only under the doctor's supervision and never in early pregnancy.

ROOIBOS

Aspalanthus linearis

Rooibos is one of South Africa's best-known exports. It is fascinating to think that the Bushmen and Hottentots used it as a medicinal drink in the early centuries, but commercial exploitation of rooibos began only in the first part of the 20th century.

Long ago, the Capoid people, who inhabited the Cederberg area where rooibos grows naturally, were the first to discover the exceptional qualities of rooibos. They gathered it and prepared it by chopping it up, crushing it with a wooden mallet and drying it in the hot summer sun. Even then it was a good bartering commodity, and later, in 1904, Benjamin Ginsberg began marketing the tea gathered wild, and it started a trend.

In 1948 the Clanwilliam Co-operative Tea Company was established, and it flourishes to this day, with intensive cultivation of rooibos in the area where it flourishes—the Cederberg. Inexpensive and easily available, it has long been a favourite drink, and with its tonic, health-giving properties, rooibos is a household name, a favourite everywhere.

Brew it to your favourite strength, add it cooled to fruit juices, jellies, cakes, sauces, stews, and even cosmetics, or have it as a wonderfully relaxing tea, weak and black, with a slice of lemon, sweetened if liked with a little honey. I add a sprig of lavender or a sprig of lemon balm, which is delicious and helps to wind one down at the end of a frantic day.

For allergies, liver and bladder disorders, flu, coughs and colds, tension, nausea, headaches and as a health drink, rooibos holds the crown!

RASPBERRY ICED TEA

The summer bounty of fruit makes this a stunning tea as a lunchtime refresher and it will ease so many little problems—we should be elegantly sipping it often.

1 large raspberry leaf
18 fruits
a stick of cinnamon
2 cloves
1 teaspoon of lemon zest
2 slices of cucumber
sprig of fresh mint

Take the large raspberry leaf with 6 fruits, cinnamon and cloves. Pour over this 1 cup of boiling water, add lemon zest and stir well. Stand for 5 minutes. Strain and cool. Now add 12 more raspberries and cucumber and fresh mint. Whirl in a liquidiser. Add ice. Serve chilled. It's refreshingly unusual and delicious! You can add honey if liked.

ROOIBOS HEALTH TEA

This is my favourite way of drinking rooibos. Hot or chilled, it's not only delicious but it's good for everything.

1 teaspoon or 1 teabag of rooibos
1 slice of fresh lemon and a good squeeze of lemon juice
3 thin slices of fresh ginger
3 cloves
2 sprigs of lemon balm leaves or a thumb-length
sprig of spearmint

Take rooibos, fresh lemon and lemon juice, fresh ginger, cloves and lemon balm or spearmint. Pour over everything 2 cups of boiling water, stand for 5 minutes, strain. Sweeten with a touch of honey. Pour 1 cup hot and sip slowly and keep the rest in the fridge for later and have it cold with ice.

Rose and rosehip

Rosa species

It's worth growing a few old-fashioned roses just for those pretty vibrant orange rosehips in autumn—which can be crushed and dried for year-round use—and it's worth using those old-fashioned rose petals for an old-fashioned rose tea.

Our grandmothers added fresh rose petals (always unsprayed and organically grown) to ordinary tea or made into a fragrant tea to ease tension, over-tiredness, stress, anxiety, bladder ailments, indigestion, insomnia, premenstrual tension, period pains, and anger and despair, and for those times when one feels miserable and unloved! It's a nurturing tea that works so beautifully.

There is such comfort in sipping hot rosepetal or rosehip tea when life gets to be too much for us, and the bonus is it helps to boost the immune system and fight colds, flu and the stress of fast-lane living.

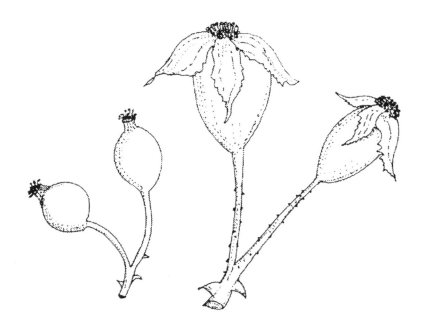

Rose Petal Tea

My favourite roses to use are the brilliant red crimson glory, or the Margaret Roberts apothecary rose or the Abraham Derby.

Add ¼ cup of rose petals to 1 cup of boiling water, stand for five minutes, then strain. Add a touch of honey and a pinch of cinnamon powder and sip slowly. It's an experience!

Rosehip Tea

Using fresh rosehips, pour 1 cup of boiling water over ¼ cup of crushed fresh rosehips and let it stand for five minutes. Stir and crush well with the spoon, strain, add a little honey and sip slowly. If you are using dried rosehips, boil ½ cup of dried crushed hips in 3 cups of water for 15 minutes with the lid on. Top up the water to the 3 cups if it boils away. Then strain and sweeten with honey (or cool and keep excess in the fridge and add fresh fruit juice for a refreshing cooldrink). Take hot during a cold or flu with a squeeze of lemon juice and a slice of fresh ginger and honey.

HOT ROSEHIP CUP FOR COLDS

A winter-time treat to boost the immune system.

¼ cup of crushed fresh rosehips

1 teaspoon of lemon zest

juice of ½ a lemon

a dash of sweet sherry

a teaspoon of honey

½ teaspoon of ginger powder or 1 teaspoon grated fresh ginger

½ teaspoon of cinnamon powder

Crush and chop rosehips. Pour over 1 cup of boiling water, add lemon zest and stand for 5 minutes. Stir well and strain. Add the lemon juice, sweet sherry, honey, ginger and cinnamon powder and mix well. Sip slowly—hot and spicy.

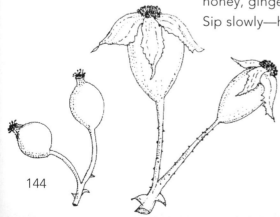

Rosella

Hibiscus sabdariffa

One of my favourite teas is the sour tasting, brilliantly red, energising tea made from the fresh or dried calyxes of the charming annual roselle, or rosella bush. This is an annual shrub with large leaves and yellow hibiscus-like flowers and produces a fruit consisting of a green seed surrounded by dark red fleshy leaves.

Rich in betacarotene and high in vitamins, specially vitamin C and vitamin D, food industries across the world are considering roselle, with its brilliant red colouring, as a substitute for tartrazine and other coal-tar colourants and dyes currently used.

Roselle originated in Malaysia and India, and the first recordings of both leaves and calyxes being used as food and medicine were found in 1687 in Java, and from there it spread to Australia and America.

It has similar properties to the American cranberry, but is far easier to grow as a quick summer annual. The large seeds can be individually planted 80 cm apart where they are to grow, or, if scattered, seedlings, when they are big enough to handle, can be easily transplanted if kept cool, shaded and moist. The bushes grow quickly and can grow up to 1 metre in height if well watered and planted with rich compost in full sun.

The roselle calyxes, reaped when the pale yellow hibiscus flowers have faded and the calyx is large and swollen, can be dried—the calyx is torn away from the large seed capsule.

Rosella tea is taken for coughs, colds and flu up to three times daily and used as a gargle for sore throats, and cooled, makes a lotion for rashes, bites and itches. Roselle contains a vast array of minerals and amino acids and such an extraordinary amount of vitamin C that it is becoming a health drink of note, and, cooled with lemon slices, makes a fabulous summer energising cooldrink. Enjoy!

ROSEMARY

Rosmarinus officinalis

Rosemary is one of the most well-known and much-loved extensively grown herbs all over the world, and its native habitat in the Mediterranean area, and Southern Europe, ensures its adaptation to moderate climates anywhere in the world.

It is easy to grow and to care for, and the many varieties make it a landscaper's dream. Its tough resilience to the extremes of weather and temperature, and its perky adaptation to storms, winds and drought give it a true place in history!

All the varieties have the same medicinal values—from the giant tough Tuscan Blue to the small, neat and compact Mountain Mist, and everything else in between, white flowers, pink flowers, dark blue and powder blue—it's all there and it's delicious!

Rosemary is an energiser of note, and its anti-inflammatory and circulatory actions are legendary. For rheumatism and arthritis it has long been respected, and for diabetes, chronic pain and long-term stress, rosemary is still one of the best treatments. Medical research has established its abundant calcium level that can be easily digested by the body, and a cup of rosemary tea—only one cup—taken daily for ten days, is usually the dose prescribed. Give it a break for three to four days, then repeat.

For the over-stressed, for falling hair and serious hair loss, for depression, anxiety, the inability to thrive, to improve memory, concentration, and to restore a positive outlook, to get up and go, and as a herbal tonic and rejuvenator and a revitaliser, rosemary is the herb! Give yourself a boost!

Rosella Flu Fighter Tea

¼ cup of fresh or dried calyxes of the rosella flower

3 slices of ginger root

¼ cup of echinacea petals and leaves

4 sage leaves

juice of ½ a lemon

honey to sweeten

Place in a cup fresh or dried calyxes of the rosella flower, ginger root, echinacea petals and leaves, sage leaves, lemon juice and lemon rind. Pour 2 cups of boiling water over everything. Stand for 5–6 minutes. Strain. Sweeten with honey. Sip ½ a cup of this brew 4 times throughout the day. Warm before sipping—it works best warm.

ROSEMARY TEA FOR HAIR

Rosemary encourages the hair to grow and to shine! This energising tea is a wonderful tonic.

1 thumb-length sprig of fresh rosemary
1 thumb-length lemon grass leaf
2 small sprigs of fresh stinging nettle
4 cloves
a twist of orange peel
a touch of honey

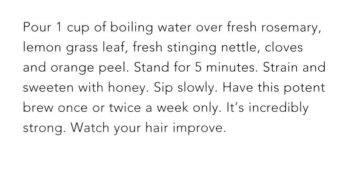

Pour 1 cup of boiling water over fresh rosemary, lemon grass leaf, fresh stinging nettle, cloves and orange peel. Stand for 5 minutes. Strain and sweeten with honey. Sip slowly. Have this potent brew once or twice a week only. It's incredibly strong. Watch your hair improve.

Rose-scented Geranium

Pelargonium graveolens

Of all the exquisitely scented pelargoniums, the rose-scented one is the favourite for a beautifully calming and relaxing tea.

It is a quick relaxant and works almost magically on the bus drivers who drive out a busload of excitedly chattering ladies to the Herbal Centre for a workshop! A cup of rose-scented geranium tea unwinds and quietens even the most frazzled!

This easy-to-grow perennial is one of South Africa's own indigenous healing plants from which a precious rose-scented oil is extracted. This oil aids stress, sleeplessness, premenstrual tension, depression and grief.

A cup of rose-scented geranium tea is still one of the world's best medicinal teas, relaxing the whole digestive and nervous system: 3 leaves (equal to ¼ of a cup) in 1 cup of boiling water, stand for five minutes, then strain. The tea, sipped slowly, sweetened with honey if liked, will ease a headache, soothe tearfulness, stiff muscles, stomach cramps and muscle spasms and take away that feeling of helplessness and anxiety.

For someone aggressively spoiling for a fight, this is the tea that can diffuse the situation and soothe everyone else too!

Our grandmothers used bunches of the fresh leaves in the bath and under the pillow and a cup of rose-scented geranium tea before going to sleep to soothe tension, upsets and worry, worry, worry! We need to take note and remember to have a cup of calmness in the midst of our hectic days.

Grow this remarkable plant in full sun in a well-dug, well-composted area. The mature bush can reach up to 1 metre in height and almost that in width, so it makes a feature in the garden or in a large tub, offering a mass of succulently fragrant leaves for constant picking.

Rose-Scented Geranium Soothing Tea

This is for when it all gets to be too much and tearfulness and misery engulf us!

¼ cup of fresh rose-scented geranium leaves

1 cinnamon stick

6 rose petals

1 teaspoon of caraway seeds

2 allspice berries, crushed lightly

Honey to sweeten

Pour 1 cup of boiling water over rose-scented geranium leaves, cinnamon stick, petals, caraway seeds and allspice berries, crushed lightly. Stand for 5 minutes. Strain. Sweeten with honey. Sip slowly, slowly. Feel the relaxation creeping in. This is a magical tea. Drink it often, it makes the world a better place!

SAGE

Salvia officinalis

Sage is one of the most popular ancient herbs—it's been around a long time, and has been cultivated by the monks through the centuries as a medicine and a memory enhancer. Native to the Mediterranean area, sage's uses were so respected that it was cultivated in fields for use as a medicine as far back as the 5th century AD.

It has antiseptic and antifungal properties, and has long been used as a gargle for sore throats. Sage tea has been the lifesaver for winter coughs, colds, flu and bronchitis, as well as for indigestion, irregular menstruation, for premature ageing, and loss of memory in the aged. Sage has a high oestrogen content, so it is very important for the symptoms of menopause. Reliable, effective and treasured, sage is an old friend, there to pick you up when it all gets to be too much.

To make the tea, use ¼ of a cup of fresh sage leaves, pour over this 1 cup of boiling water and leave it to stand for five minutes. Strain, sweeten with honey, add a slice of lemon and sip slowly. Take one cup a day and after ten days give it a break of two to three days, then repeat. Use the cooled tea as a wash for acne, as a gargle for a sore throat and mouth infection, and as a wash for rashes, grazes and rough skin. Grow sage in full sun in light, well-drained soil and water only once a week—it doesn't like wet feet.

A pretty perennial, it grows into a neat small bush and its spring abundance of mauve flowers can be added to this comforting and very effective tea. The butterflies love it too!

Sage and Peppermint Exam-time Tea

These two herbs help us to retain facts and enhance our memory and although they both have powerful flavours, they combine beautifully. Use Mentha piperita nigra–this is the dark, almost red-black-stemmed peppermint.

¼ cup of fresh sage leaves
1 thumb-length sprig of peppermint
a little honey
a squeeze of lemon juice

Take fresh sage leaves and of peppermint. Pour over this 1 cup of boiling water. Stand for 5 minutes, strain. Sweeten with a little honey and add a squeeze of lemon juice. Sip slowly. During exam times take 2 cups daily. As a tonic and brainpower tea take 1 cup daily for 10 days, then stop for 3 or 4 days, then continue.

STEVIA

Stevia rebaudiana

Stevia is the sweetest herb in all the world – 300 times sweeter than sugar! It originated in South America, and in our trials at the Herbal Centre over the past few years it has adapted well to South African conditions and now is available at most nurseries for those who want this amazing plant near at hand.

A sprig of stevia, enough to fill ½ a cup, with 1 cup of boiling water poured over it, must be left to draw after bruising the leaves. Stand for five minutes, then strain. Pleasantly sweet and with a remarkably sweet aftertaste, this extraordinary tea will help to lower high blood pressure, high blood cholesterol and high blood sugar as well as fight tooth decay and plaque, and research continues.

It has long been used in its land of origin for treating sore throats, bleeding gums, fever blisters and mouth sores. Use the cooled tea as a gargle – it has antibacterial properties. Stevia is completely non-toxic and new research seems to suggest that it has a strengthening effect on the heart and the cardiovascular system.

What is most astonishing of all about stevia is that it is a low-calorie sweetener, rather like a natural sweetener that does not affect blood glucose levels – so it is safe for diabetics.

Fresh stevia leaves can be added to any other herb teas as a natural sweetener, anything from two finely chopped leaves to a whole sprig. It is the bruising, the chopping and the chewing that releases the steviocide that gives that incredible sweetness.

A fairly hardy perennial, stevia likes full sun and well-dug, well-composted soil and a deep watering twice or even three times a week. It dies down in winter and sends luscious honey-sweet, tender leaves out in spring, waiting to be chewed as natural candy!

STEVIA AND ROSELLA TONIC

This tea is superb for throat infections and for debilitating over-tiredness.

Take ¼ cup of fresh or dried rosella calyxes, ¼ cup of crushed, chopped stevia sprigs, 1 teaspoon of lemon zest, 2 cups of water and 2 tablespoons of fresh or dried elderberries. Simmer everything together gently in a stainless-steel pot for 15 minutes – keep it covered. Top up the water if necessary. Strain. Sip about ½ a cup two or three times through the day for flu and throat infections. Take once a day for 10 days for fatigue, then stop. Check with your doctor.

St John's wort

Hypericum perforatum

First, be one hundred per cent sure you have the right variety. There are many St John's worts and it is only this small-leafed one that is the medicinal St John's wort.

It originated in Britain and Europe where it has been used for centuries as a potent medicinal plant and much has been written and recorded, and now medical research is verifying its superb actions. Some claim that this is nature's Prozac, and it certainly is a most important herb for nervous problems, depression, anxiety, panic attacks and hormonal change, menstrual problems, menopause, tension, sleeplessness, decreased energy and vitality. It is also an excellent tonic for the liver and gall bladder.

Capsules and tinctures are available at the pharmacy as well as health shops, but there is something wonderfully satisfying in picking your own flowers for tea. Use the fresh flowering tops and a few little leaves, enough to make ¼ cup, pour 1 cup of boiling water over this and let it stand and steep for five minutes. Then strain, sweeten with honey if liked and sip slowly. Take once a day no for longer than ten days, then stop. Give it a break for five days, then start again if necessary.

Interestingly, this precious tea is being tested for over-sensitive, over-tired students, suffering from burn-out, with positive results, and for students under stress during exam times, the favourable results are worth thinking about.

A little goes a long way with this herb. Treat it with respect and discuss using it with your doctor for long-term treatments.

St John's Wort Mood-uplifting Tea

¼ cup of fresh flowering tops of St John's wort

¼ cup rose-scented geranium leaves

1 thumb-length lavender flower

a touch of honey

Pour 1 cup of boiling water over ¼ cup of fresh flowering tops of St John's wort, ¼ cup rose-scented geranium leaves and 1 thumb-length lavender flower. Stand for 5 minutes, strain. Sweeten with a touch of honey and sip slowly. This is a most soothing, comforting tea that helps you to unwind and feel better. It unravels a tense situation and lifts the spirits. We all need this peace-making tea!

STINGING NETTLE

Urtica dioica

Who could think the feared and avoided stinging nettle could be so important a health-giving tea?

A waste-ground weed in temperate regions worldwide, the formic acid on the tiny hairs on the leaves and stems causes the burning or stinging sensation, and its tough resilient nature ensures its spread–so walk carefully. The soothing juice of Bulbine frutescens will quickly deaden the sting–so always grow bulbinella near it.

Steamed as a spinach (pick with gloves on), nettle is packed with minerals and vitamins, and makes a delicious and nourishing meal served with butter and black pepper, and a tea made by pouring 1 cup boiling water over ¼ cup fresh nettle sprigs (the hot water immediately takes the sting out), makes the most marvellous health booster.

Nettle's key actions are cleansing and detoxifying, and that is why it is so essential for treating arthritis, gout, bladder and urinary infections, poor kidney function, and fluid retention. Nettle is a marvellous diuretic and thus it increases urine flow and dissolves blockages in the urethra.

It is also an excellent anti-allergenic, and it eases hay fever, asthma, eczema and insect bites, rashes and itches, and it helps to reduce enlarged and inflamed prostate. Nettle tea for breastfeeding mothers is a great help and it purifies the blood, eases and clears and dissolves bronchial catarrh, it will stimulate hair growth and give lustre and strength to the hair, clear dandruff from the scalp, stop internal haemorrage, aid the healing of the liver in jaundice, aid infertility, dysentery and anaemia.

Take one cup of nettle tea daily for ten days, then stop for two days, then continue for ten days and so on. Find a place in the sun for this miraculous plant!

STRAWBERRY

Fragaria vesca

Who would have thought the much loved and easy-to-grow strawberry is an important medicinal plant?

The fruit has been a popular cosmetic remedy and liver tonic for centuries, and if you think that the wild strawberry, from which all the varieties have arisen, was used in ancient times as a treatment for diarrhoea, colic and digestive upsets, gout and arthritis, you can be assured the strawberry has stood the tests of time.

Modern research reveals that the fruit and the leaves are packed with minerals, vitamins and salicylates, and that a tea made from ¼ cup of leaves with a couple of ripe strawberries in season, topped with 1 cup of boiling water and left to steep for five minutes, then strained, can be taken for all the above as well as kidney infections, urinary tract infections and even diabetes.

The strawberry—all parts of it, including the flowers—are rich in antioxidants and destroy many viruses, including herpes simplex, and will benefit the whole cardiovascular system.

Because of their pectin and fibre content the berries help to reduce high blood pressure, and polyphenols in the fruit and the leaves fight cancer. Crushed fruit has been used since the early centuries for skin cancer, poultices and for skin eruptions. So the tea of fruit and leaves, cooled and strained, is also a fabulous beauty aid as both a rinse and a mist spray.

Easy to grow and prolific in the garden, it is so worthwhile growing your own strawberries in full sun with richly composted soil as an edging plant.

Stinging Nettle Tea

This is the most soothingly marvellous tea for those aches and pains and it's great for your ageing dog too! Add the tea to your dog's food or drinking water.

¼ cup of fresh nettle sprigs
a piece of cinnamon bark
lemon juice or honey to taste

Pour 1 cup of boiling water over nettle sprigs and cinnamon bark and stand for 5 minutes. Strain. Sip slowly–best is without honey or lemon juice but add either or both to give better taste. Drink 1 cup a day for 10 days, then give it a 2–3 day break, then continue.

STRAWBERRY LEAF TEA

*This is an old-fashioned, much-respected remedy for bladder
ailments.*

¼ cup of fresh strawberry leaves
¼ cup of goldenrod flowers and a few leaves
1 teaspoon of lemon zest
¼ cup of corn silk, fresh or dried
juice of 1 lemon
honey to sweeten
2 or 3 ripe strawberries

Take fresh strawberry leaves, goldenrod flowers
and a few leaves (dry the autumn-flowering sprigs
before they are fully open for all-year-round use),
lemon zest and corn silk. Simmer everything
together in 2 cups of water for 6–7 minutes. Cool
and strain. Add lemon juice and honey and 2 or 3
ripe strawberries. Take ¼ cup 4–6 times through the
day.

Tea tree

Melaleuca alternifolia

This is the real thing, the Australian tea tree, and very well worth sitting up and taking notice of! Now that the growers are getting such excellent results in propagating the tricky-to-grow tea tree, everyone can grow it, but not in the very cold areas.

It grows to roof height in three years and thrives with being cut back to knee height yearly, producing masses of feathery soft branches of needle-like leaves richly laced with the incredible tea tree oil, waiting to be experienced.

Tea tree really is worth getting excited about. It is an effective antibacterial, antifungal and antiviral plant. It is a potent medicine, an exciting cosmetic, and an effective natural insect repellent, and there literally is no end to its fascinating uses.

A tea of fresh tea tree sprigs for both acute and chronic conditions is a quick way to experience its efficacy. Take ¼ cup of fresh sprigs, pour over this 1 cup of boiling water and stand for five minutes. Strain and sip slowly, sweeten with honey if liked, or cool and add fresh fruit juice.

Tea tree is excellent for treating glandular fever, cystitis, coughs, colds, flu, bronchitis, headaches, aches and pains. It acts as a natural anti-inflammatory, is effective against parasites, but is non-toxic, non-irritant, antiseptic, and it acts as a general revitaliser, energiser and tonic.

The cooled tea will soothe insect bites, red sore wind- and sunburned skin, and in a mist spray bottle will refresh and restore good humour on the hottest day.

No wonder the Australians are so mad about tea tree. It's really something special. Plant the tree in full sun in a compost-filled hole and nurture it!

TURMERIC

Curcuma longa syn C. domestica

Few people realise the amazing medicinal values of this familiar spicy yellow-coloured powder. Much loved in curry mixes in India and Asia, where it originated, turmeric's therapeutic actions have only recently been researched and understood.

Much interest has been ignited by the abilities of turmeric to lower high blood cholesterol, to aid in cancer prevention, and in its anti-inflammatory actions. Interestingly, the ancient Greeks used turmeric to create yellow dyes, and the Chinese physicians used turmeric 3 000 years ago to treat arthritis, liver and chest conditions, and recent medical research has proved its extraordinary properties.

Turmeric has anti-coagulant abilities which ease the circulation and lessen the pain in arthritic swellings, it has the marvellous actions of soothing psoriasis, eczema and fungal infections, and it helps to repair and tone the liver.

Asthma sufferers find relief with turmeric tea to which 1 teaspoon of aniseed is added, and, as a digestive herb, turmeric eases sour belching, nausea, flatulence, bloating, gastritis, heartburn and general over-acidity.

Still more research is ongoing for turmeric as a protective remedy for those at risk of developing cancer, and a cup of turmeric tea on alternate days is being recommended by some doctors to lower the risk of a stroke.

To make the tea, add 1 teaspoon of turmeric powder to 1 cup of boiling water. Stir briskly, then sip slowly. Take 1 cup a day for ten days, then give it a break for two to four days, then continue. Some doctors suggest eating a biscuit or a rusk with the tea to help absorb the brilliant colour, but it is the bright golden colour that contains the benefit!

Tea Tree and Olive Leaf Flu and Bronchitis Tea

This tea will help to fight infections and is a superb anti-inflammatory. Think of that aching back and that cystitis as you sip this tea.

¼ cup of fresh tea tree sprigs

¼ cup of olive leaf sprigs

honey to sweeten

a squeeze of lemon juice to taste

Take tea tree sprigs and olive leaf sprigs. Pour over this 1 cup of boiling water. Stand for 4 minutes. Strain. Sip slowly. Take 1 cup two or even three times a day during the infection. As a chronic tea take 1 cup a day. Sweeten with honey and add lemon juice if liked.

Tea Tree (left) and Olive Sprigs (right)

Turmeric with Tea Tree

This combination of tea tree and turmeric is simply amazing! It has a tonic effect on the whole system and combined with stinging nettle is a powerful tea to liver toning.

¼ cup of tea tree sprigs
¼ cup of stinging nettle sprigs
1 teaspoon of aniseed
1 teaspoon of turmeric powder
a squeeze of lemon

Pour 1 cup of boiling water over tea tree sprigs, stinging nettle sprigs, aniseed and turmeric powder. Stand for 5 minutes, stir well. Strain. Sip slowly with a squeeze of lemon and relish its brilliant yellowness. Remember turmeric stains—sip with care!

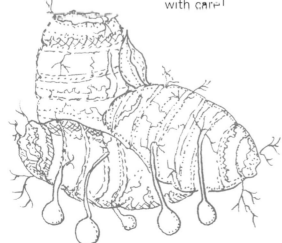

VIOLET

Viola odorata

The nostalgically beautiful little garden violet has been a favourite herb through the centuries across Asia and Europe, where it is indigenous, and beyond. Small, quite unobtrusive and with such astonishing healing abilities, this much-loved little plant goes back in history to the first century AD, when it was recorded as an important medicinal plant.

Grown in both palace gardens and cottage gardens the world over, the little violet adapted and flourished and made history first with the ancient Greeks who so respected it they made it the symbol of Athens, and then later with Napoleon–it was his favourite flower and he gave violets to Josephine on their wedding day and on every anniversary, and finally planted them on her grave.

There are recordings of the violet being used in Syria, Turkey and North Africa as a medicinal tea in the earliest centuries, and violet flowers steeped in honey were a traditional treatment for hay fever and headaches even then.

During the Middle Ages the monks made liqueurs and meads with violets as a treatment for colds, coughs and flu. Warmed and very potent, and enticingly fragrant, a few sips so soothed aching throats and congested chests that rows and rows of violets were grown in the monastery gardens.

Leaves, flowers and even the roots all contain soothing mucilage that acts as a decongestant in the lungs and throat, opens blocked sinuses, and dissipates streaming hay fever, sneezing, headaches, and even itchy eyes. Make the tea by pouring 1 cup of boiling water over ¼ cup fresh violet flowers and leaves and leave it to stand for five minutes. Stir in a little honey if liked, then strain and sip slowly.

Violets have a long-time reputation for treating tumours, both benign and cancerous, and a cup of violet tea daily is often comfortingly effective, under the guidance of the doctor.

Yarrow

Achillea millefolium

This ancient and revered perennial cottage garden herb was once known as 'Herba Militaris' and its leaves were used to staunch battleground wounds. Achilles used yarrow to heal the warriors' wounds during the Battle of Troy, hence its Latin name Achillea, and the Crusaders took it, along with borage, to treat their wounds on their journeys.

Through the centuries yarrow has been used to treat high blood pressure, to reduce fever, to heal wounds and to stop internal bleeding, and modern-day research verifies that indeed it does all that as well as regulating the menstrual cycle, improving the circulatory system, it is a superb anti-inflammatory and urinary antiseptic, and has the marvellous ability to help recovery after an illness.

Yarrow has antispasmodic, astringent and antibacterial properties, and it will beautifully and effectively ease premenstrual tension, water retention and mouth infections.

A tea can be made by pouring 1 cup of boiling water over ¼ cup of fresh yarrow leaves and a few of the pretty pink and white flowers. Leave it to stand for five minutes, then strain, sweeten with a touch of honey if liked and sip slowly. Take one to two or even three cups a day for treating acute conditions like chicken pox or measles, or one cup a day for chronic conditions such as rheumatism, diabetes, high blood pressure and nose bleeds. Use the tea as a wash for grazes, scratches, rashes, cuts and scrapes, and for clearing flu, colds and coughs.

Take the tea for no more than seven days continuously, then give it a break for seven days, then continue.

NOTE: Use only the old-fashioned pink and white yarrow (young flowers are pink, which fade to white as they age).

Violet Tea for Sinus Congestion

¼ cup of fresh violet leaves and a few flowers
¼ cup of sage leaves
¼ cup of bergamot leaves
¼ cup of tea tree sprigs
2 teaspoons of aniseed
squeeze of lemon juice

Take fresh violet leaves and a few flowers if you can find them, sage leaves, bergamot leaves and tea tree sprigs. Simmer all together with aniseed in 3 cups of water for 10 minutes. Cool. Strain. Add a squeeze of lemon juice if liked. Sip ½ a cup twice or even three times a day, warmed, to relieve the sinus congestion. (Also steam with several drops of tea tree oil and eucalyptus oil under a towel tent over a steaming pot of water.)

Yarrow, Fennel and Parsley for PMT

Beautifully antispasmodic, this fabulous tea will take away pre-menstrual water retention, bloatedness and improve the circulation, and make you feel better!

¼ cup of fresh yarrow leaves
¼ cup of fresh fennel leaves
¼ cup of fresh parsley
juice of ½ a lemon

Take yarrow leaves, fennel leaves and fresh parsley. Add 2 cups of boiling water and lemon juice. Stand for 5 minutes, then strain. Sip slowly, about 2/3 of a cup 3 times or more during the day.

CHOCOLATE MINT SPECIAL TEA

I leave the best until last to say goodbye, in the hope that these teas throughout this little book will have given you new thoughts, new tastes, new health and lots of new interest.

There is a special mint called Chocolate Mint that literally tastes like a peppermint crisp and it is such a fabulous tea to sip at the end of a meal. I serve it often, and also drop a leaf into the occasional cup of filter coffee friends ask for at the end of a meal, those who are not yet used to the herbal teas. Try it for a taste experience. It will amaze you and it will also smooth, soothe and ease any indigestion or a feeling of fullness.

Do this for a rare and special occasion:

1/4 cup fresh chocolate mint sprigs
1 peppermint chocolate bar (Peppermint Crisp is best!)

Pour the water over the mint sprigs and stir with the peppermint chocolate bar—it will start to melt into the tea. Remove the sprigs and eat the peppermint crisp and sip the tea. This is a sure way to start even the most skeptical thinking about herb teas. Enjoy.

Ailment chart

A

abdominal distention *see bloating*

aching joints *celery, comfrey, rosemary, St John's wort*

aching muscles *chamomile, ginger, marjoram, rose scented geranium*

acidity *chamomile, fennel, mint*

acne *buchu, cloves, comfrey. parsley, rosella*

adaptogenic *basil*

alcoholism *lucerne, lemon balm*

allergies *echinacea, rooibos*

analgesic *buchu, clover, cloves, lavender*

anorexia *cardamom*

anti-ageing *borage, celery, lemon thyme, lucerne*

anti-allergenic *chamomile, echinacea, stinging nettle*

antibacterial *calendula, cinnamon, green tea, lavender, marjoram, olive leaf, stevia, tea tree, turmeric*

antibiotic *buchu, echinacea, lucerne, rosemary, sage*

anti-cancer *clover, green tea, lemon, turmeric*

anticoagulant *turmeric*

antidepressant *jasimine, lavender, lemon verbena, lemon balm, oat straw, olive leaf, rose hip, rosemary, St John's wort*

antifungal *calendula, comfrey, marjoram, tea tree*

anti-inflammatory *basil, bergamot, chamomile, clover, echinacea, ginger, lemon, rose hip, rosemary, sage, tea tree, yarrow*

anti-oxidant *green tea, lemon, turmeric*

anti-rheumatic *borage, chamomile, comfrey*

antiseptic *bergamot, calendula, cloves, ginger, lavender, rose hip,* tea tree, yarrow

antispasmodic *anise, basil, cardamom, chamomile, cinnamon, cloves, lemon thyme, lemon verbena, marjoram, lemon balm, rose hip, rosemary, St John's wort, yarrow*

antiviral *echinacea, lemon balm, olive oil, rose hip, St John's wort, tea tree*

anxiety *lavender, lucerne, marjoram, lemon balm, mint, oat straw, rose-scented geranium*

aphrodisiac *cardamom*

appetite, poor *nutmeg*

arthritis *catmint, celery, clover, comfrey, elderflower, lemon grass, linseed, lucerne, parsley, stinging nettle, strawberry, turmeric*

asthma *anise, cardamom, chamomile, cinnamon, echinacea, lemon thyme, maidenhair fern, stinging nettle, turmeric*

astringent *calendula, green tea, lemon, rose hip, rosella, rosemary, sage, strawberry, yarrow*

athlete's foot *buchu, calendula, marjoram*

B

bed sores *comfrey*

bedwetting *catmint, marjoram*

bladder ailments *borage, buchu, cardamom, celery, fennel, goldenrod, linseed, maidenhair fern, parsley, rooibos*

bleeding gums *stevia*

bloating *anise, buchu, caraway, chamomile, fennel, lavender, marjoram, mint, nutmeg*

blocked ears *comfrey, echinacea, mullein, violet*

blood sugar, lowering *basil, olive leaf*

blood tonic *basil, clover, lemon, lucerne, rose hip*

boils *comfrey, echinacea, lucerne, mealie silk*

brain power, *peppermint, sage*

breast cancer *clover, violet*

breast milk production, increases *caraway, lucerne, stinging nettle*

breast milk production, reduces *sage*

breastfeeding, aid to *fennel*

breath sweetener *anise, caraway, cardamom, parsley, mint*

bronchitis *anise, cardamom, clover, comfrey, echinacea, linseed, mullein, tea tree, violet*

bruises *comfrey, marjoram*

C

catarrh *elderflower, golden rod, maidenhair fern, violet*

chest infections *comfrey, echinacea, lemon thyme, linseed, lucerne, mullein, violet*

chilblains *echinacea, ginger*

chills *echinacea, ginger, lucerne*

cholesterol, high *basil, celery, fennel, green tea, parsley, stevia, turmeric*

chronic fatigue syndrome *olive leaf*

circulation, poor *ginger, rosemary, yarrow*

cleansing *basil, celery, fennel, mealie silk, parsley, stinging nettle*

cold hands *ginger, lucerne*

cold sores *see fever blisters*

colds *bergamot, echinacea, elder flower, ginger, green tea, lemon thyme, maidenhair fern, marjoram, pineapple sage, rooibos, rose hip, rosella, tea tree, violet, yarrow*

colic *anise, caraway, cardamom, catmint, chamomile, fennel, lemon grass, lemon verbena, linseed, lemon balm, mint, rose hip, strawberry*

colitis *calendula, lemon balm, mint*

congestion *buchu, comfrey, ginger, lucerne, mullein, sage, violet*

constipation *linseed*

coughs *anise, bergamot, borage, buchu, clover, comfrey, elderflower, ginger, green tea, lemon thyme, maidenhair fern, marjoram, mullein, rooibos, rose hip, rosella, tea tree, violet*

cramps *lemon grass, mint*

cystitis *borage, cardamom, goldenrod, mealie silk, olive leaf, tea tree*

D

decongestant *bergamot, comfrey, echinacea, mullein, violet*

detoxifier *basil, calendula, celery, echinacea, fennel, parsley, stinging nettle*

diarrhoea *goldenrod, nutmeg, raspberry, rose hip, strawberry*

digestive tonic *anise, bergamot, calendula, caraway, cardamom, cinnamon, fennel, lemon grass, lemon verbena, linseed, lemon balm, mint, nutmeg, parsley, pineapple sage, rosemary, turmeric*

digestive upsets *bergamot, lemon balm, mint, oat straw, strawberry*

disinfectant *lavender, lemon thyme, marjoram, sage*

diuretic *borage, celery, fennel, green tea, lemon, mealie silk, olive leaf, parsley, raspberry, rosemary, stinging nettle, strawberry, yarrow*

drug addiction *lucerne*

dry skin *jasmine, oat straw, sage*

E

ear infection *echinacea, elderflower, lucerne, mullein*

earache *echinacea, mullein*

eczema *borage, chamomile, clover, elderflower, stinging nettle, turmeric*

energiser *lucerne, oat straw, peppermint, rosella, rosemary*

exhaustion *chamomile, jasmine, lavender, rose scented geranium*

expectorant *anise, borage, comfrey, fennel, lemon thyme, lemon verbena, mullein, violet*

F

fear *lemon balm, peppermint, rosemary*

fever *catmint, elderflower, ginger, lemon grass, lemon balm, olive leaf, yarrow*

fever blisters *echinacea, elderflower, peppermint, stevia*

flatulence *caraway, cardamom, catmint, lemon grass, linseed, marjoram, lemon balm, mint*

flu *buchu, echinacea, ginger, lemon balm, olive leaf, rooibos, sage, tea tree, yarrow*

fluid retention *celery, fennel, mealie silk, parsley*

fractures *comfrey*

frigidity *anise*

fungal infections *comfrey, echinacea, turmeric*

G

gastric ulcer *calendula, lemon balm*

gastritis *chamomile, lemon balm, oat straw*

gastroenteritis *goldenrod*

glandular fever *tea tree*

gout *clover, comfrey, fennel, parsley, stinging nettle, strawberry*

grief *lavender, lemon balm, oat straw*

gripe *anise, cardamom, caraway, lemon balm*

H

haemorrhoids *catmint*

hay fever *bergamot, chamomile, elderflower, stinging nettle, violet*

headache *catmint, ginger, rooibos, tea tree, violet*

heart tonic *rosemary, stevia*

heartburn *anise, buchu, caraway, fennel, lemon grass, linseed, lemon balm, mint, nutmeg, pineapple sage*

high blood pressure *basil, celery, green tea, lemon, olive leaf, stevia, yarrow*

high blood sugar *basil, olive leaf, stevia*

HIV/Aids *echinacea*

hot flushes *goldenrod, sage*

hyperactivity *lavender, lemon balm, oat straw, rose scented geranium*

I

immune system, booster *echinacea, green tea, lemon thyme, olive leaf, sage*

impotence *anise*

incontinence *buchu, cardamom*

indigestion *bergamot, catmint, chamomile, ginger, lemon thyme*

inflammation *borage, elderflower*

insect bites *tea tree*

internal bleeding *yarrow*

irritable bowel syndrome *borage, oat straw*

itchy skin *elderflower, olive leaf, stinging nettle*

J

jaundice *maidenhair fern, turmeric*

K

kidney ailments *buchu, cardamom, celery, fennel, goldenrod,* linseed, parsley, rose hip

kidney stones fennel, goldenrod, maidenhair fern, mealie silk, rose hip

kidney tonic cinnamon, fennel, mealie silk, parsley, rose hip

L

leprosy lucerne

liver tonic basil, cinnamon, rooibos, St John's wort, strawberry, turmeric

low blood pressure rosemary

M

menopause cinnamon, lucerne, sage, St John's wort

menstrual problems lucerne

menstruation, irregular borage, parsley, yarrow

menstruation, painful anise, parsley

morning sickness chamomile, fennel, lemon, lemon balm, oat straw

mouth sores stevia

mouth ulcers raspberry, sage

multiple sclerosis oat straw, olive leaf

muscle aches comfrey, St John's wort

muscle building lucerne, rosemary

muscle spasms calendula, cloves, lavender, lemon thyme, nutmeg, sage

N

nasal congestion bergamot, cloves, mullein, violet

nausea anise, bergamot, buchu, catmint, ginger, mint, nutmeg, rooibos, turmeric

nerve tonic lemon, lemon verbena, lemon balm, oat straw, rosemary

nosebleed *stinging nettle*

O
oestrogenic *clover, oat straw, sage*
oily skin *basil, bergamot, lucerne, oat straw*
osteoporosis *comfrey, oat straw, parsley, sage*
overactive thyroid *lemon balm*
overeating *lemon balm, mint*

P
pain *relieving chamomile, cloves, oat straw, St John's wort*
pale complexion *ginger*
panic attacks *lavender, lemon balm, oat straw, rose scented
     geranium*
parasites *basil, cloves, tea tree*
plaque *stevia*
pleurisy *buchu, echinacea, ginger, marjoram*
pneumonia *comfrey, echinacea, mullein*
poor concentration *peppermint, sage*
poor memory *cloves, lucerne, peppermint, sage*
post nasal drip *clover, maidenhair fern, sage, violet*
premenstrual tension *yarrow*
prostate problems *mealie silk, raspberry, stinging nettle*
psoriasis *clover, parsley, turmeric*

R
rabies *echinacea*
rashes *calendula, comfrey, elderflower, olive leaf*
relaxing *chamomile, jasmine, lavender, lemon balm, rooibos,
     rose scented geranium*

respiratory ailments *green tea, linseed*

rheumatism *buchu, catmint, celery, comfrey, nutmeg, oat straw, parsley, raspberry, strawberry*

S

scalp problems *maidenhair fern, rosemary, stinging nettle*

scars *comfrey*

sedative *chamomile, jasmine, lavender, lemon balm, oat straw,, St John's wort*

shortness of breath *comfrey, maidenhair fern*

sinus headache *mullein, violet*

sinuses, blocked *mullein, violet*

sinusitis *clover*

skin disorders *calendula, comfrey, lucerne, nutmeg*

skin ulcers *comfrey*

sore gums *echinacea, sage*

sore nipples *calendula, chamomile, comfrey*

sore throat *elderflower, fennel, green tea, lemon, lemon thyme, maidenhair fern, pineapple sage, raspberry, rosella, sage, stevia*

sprains *comfrey*

stiffness *comfrey*

stimulant *cloves, rosemary*

stomach ache *buchu, fennel, ginger*

stomach cancer *violet*

stomach upsets *caraway, catmint, lemon balm*

stress *basil, jasmine, lavender, oat straw, rose scented geranium*

sunburn *olive leaf, tea tree*

swollen joints *comfrey, turmeric*

T

tension *basil, cloves, green tea, jasmine, lemon balm, mint, rooibos, rose scented geranium*

thrush *goldenrod*

tight chest *anise, bergamot, lemon thyme, mullein*

tired eyes *chamomile*

tonic *cinnamon, lemon thyme, rooibos, rosemary, sage, tea tree*

tonsillitis *comfrey, echinacea, marjoram*

toothache *cloves*

tooth decay *stevia*

torn ligaments *comfrey*

U

ulcers *comfrey*

urinary ailments *basil, celery, cinnamon, fennel, goldenrod, green tea, linseed, parsley, rose hip*

V

varicose veins *yarrow*

vomiting *bergamot, lemon, mint*

W

warming *ginger*

weak pulse *ginger, lucerne*

weight loss *celery, fennel, parsley*

whooping cough *anise, clover*

wind *anise, caraway, catmint, chamomile, lavender, mint, lemon balm*

wounds *comfrey, yarrow*

wind burn *tea tree*

First Published by Struik Nature
(an imprint of Random House Struik) in 2008

First published in Australia in 2011
by New Holland Publishers (Australia)
1/66 Gibbes Street, Chatswood NSW 2067

Publisher: Fiona Schultz
Publishing manager and editor Australian edition: Lliane Clarke
Designer: Emma Gough
Illustrations: Margaret Roberts
Photography and styling: Emma Gough (Cover shot and pages 2, 6,
      9,10,13,14,20, 24, 27, 28, 34, 37, 41, 42, 46, 49, 56, 60, 67, 70, 79,
      85, 86, 88, 93, 97, 105, 107, 108, 111, 112, 116, 119, 124, 131, 137,
      138, 141, 142, 151, 152, 155, 156, 168, 179, 192); Lizotte Jonker
      and Margaret Roberts (pages 19, 30, 34, 41, 52, 63, 68, 75, 80, 89,
      98, 102, 123, 128, 145, 148, 159, 161, 167, 176, 181)
Production manager: Olga Dementiev
Printer: Toppan Leefung (China)

A record of this book is held in the National Library of Australia
ISBN: 9781742570983

Thank you to Michelle Leonard for the Manuka Honey and Lemon Myrtle
recipe for singers. Thank you to Connie Vahldiek and Bev Jan for their
advice and to Rochelle Fernandez, Ishbel Thorpe, Talina McKenzie, Olga
Dementiev, Margot Gough and Fiona Schultz for their tea cups and pots.

Warning
Never use any plant as a tea unless you are one hundred per cent sure
of its identification. Many plants are poisonous; in some cases certain
parts of a plant may be edible, while other parts may be poisonous.
When in doubt, leave out. The author and publishers take no responsibil-
ity for any poisoning, illness or discomfort that may result from information contained in this book or due to the incorrect identification of a
plant. You are strongly advised to consult a medical practitioner before
treating yourself or your family with home remedies.